THE
ENTRANCE
INTO THE KINGDOM

THE
ENTRANCE

INTO THE KINGDOM

Holy Spirit Invitation to Intimacy

Wayne Vermeer

XULON PRESS

Xulon Press
2301 Lucien Way #415
Maitland, FL 32751
407.339.4217
www.xulonpress.com

Unless otherwise indicated, Scripture quotations taken from the Holy Bible, New International Version (NIV). Copyright © 1973, 1978, 1984, 2011 by Biblica, Inc.™. Used by permission. All rights reserved.

Scripture quotations taken from the New King James Version (NKJV). Copyright © 1982 by Thomas Nelson, Inc. Used by permission. All rights reserved.

Scripture quotations taken from the New American Standard Bible (NASB). Copyright © 1960, 1962, 1963, 1968, 1971, 1972, 1973, 1975, 1977, 1995 by The Lockman Foundation. Used by permission. All rights reserved.

Scripture quotations taken from the Amplified Bible (AMP). Copyright © 1954, 1958, 1962, 1964, 1965, 1987 by The Lockman Foundation. Used by permission. All rights reserved.

Scripture quotations taken from the Holy Bible, New Living Translation (NLT). Copyright ©1996, 2004, 2007 by Tyndale House Foundation. Used by permission of Tyndale House Publishers, Inc.

Printed in the United States of America.

Paperback ISBN-13: 978-1-6322-1499-7
eBook ISBN-13: 978-1-6322-1500-0

DEDICATION

This book is dedicated to the Holy Spirit.

Without the work of the Holy Spirit,
this book would not be possible.

Jesus said, "But very truly I tell you, it is for your good that I am going away. Unless I go away, the Advocate will not come to you; but if I go, I will send Him to you" (John 16:7; NIV).

Jesus said, "Wait for the gift my Father promised, which you have heard me speak about. For John baptized with water, but in a few days you will be baptized with the Holy Spirit" (Acts 1:4–5; NIV).

Jesus said, "But you will receive power when the Holy Spirit comes on you: and you will be my witnesses …to the ends of the earth" (Acts 1:8; NIV).

"In the last days, God says, I will pour out my Spirit on all people. Your sons and daughters will prophesy, your young men will see visions, your old men will dream dreams. Even on my servants, both men and women, I will pour out my Spirit in those days, and they will prophesy" (Acts 2:17–18; NIV).

ENDORSEMENTS

THE ENTRANCE into the Kingdom is clearly a divine initiative to prepare us for the times ahead. Wayne Vermeer is a vessel called, chosen, and forged in the crucible of a system even now struggling for identity in a post-modern world. As he puts it himself, he started attending church from "conception," and there are many who can testify to the transformation he has been through, including some older, peers of his, and many younger, a number of whom he has mentored and yet ministers with. Talk of a "cloud of witnesses" here below!

In a season when I longed for a prayer partner, God brought Wayne. He came asking me to mentor him! "He must be joking," I thought, but he was in earnest, and I knew that this was the wonderful way God chose to answer my prayer for a prayer partner. Wayne is a gift from God – a very humble and unassuming man.

I recommend that in reading this book, you must "gird up the loins of your mind and heart" and be prepared to follow scripture where it leads, It will test your love and dedication to Truth. (Jn. 14:6)

Effiong O. E. Bassey, DVM, Ph.D.

Wayne has been a spiritual father to me for many years. He was also my high school math teacher, and his wife was my kindergarten teacher! This book has been a blessing to our whole family! Our teenage daughters loved reading it too. It's packed with scripture and carries truths; the body of Christ needs to hear today. It truly is an amazing book for such a time as this!

Erica Schut, a stay-at-home mom, works from home for her husband, Greg, and a former member of the Katelyn's Fund board

Wayne has been a rock and spiritual father to me and so many others in this region. Wayne is always a man who stands first and foremost on the word of the Lord and the truth of scripture. In Wayne's book, you will see his passion for the Lord and truth; to be unlocked for all of the body of Christ. I am moved by the way this father figure follows the Holy Spirit, and the way so much scripture is unpacked on each page! Allow the Holy Spirit to use Wayne's testimony and this book to pave a road right to the heart of the Lord!

Greg Schut, Co-owner of Firm Foundation Concrete,
Leadership and Vision Team of HOME
(House of Missions and Equipping)

Wayne Vermeer is a man who was set ablaze by the Holy Spirit in the 1970s and, for nearly 50 years, has lived as a wholehearted follower of Jesus Christ. Wayne has labored in intercession for revival in America and NW Iowa for decades, and the Holy Spirit fire that now burns in my own heart is no doubt the fruit of those prayers. This book brings together his knowledge of the Word and the power of his testimony. It is guaranteed to cause you to hunger and thirst for His Kingdom to come on earth as it is in heaven. Open your heart and read the scriptures and stories in this book and let the Holy Spirit draw you to Himself.

Lyle Schut, Co-owner of Firm Foundation Concrete,
Leadership and Vision Team of HOME
(House of Mission and Equipping)

Wayne is my brother in Jesus Christ. I have had the privilege of spending years with Wayne as my math teacher, my mentor, my spiritual brother, my roommate, my prayer partner, my friend. I have been blessed with Wayne's steadfast heart that searches after Jesus; a heart that seeks answers in the scriptures, the Holy Word of God. This book – *THE ENTRANCE* – is your chance to access the wisdom that Wayne has shared with me and so many others. The truths found in the scriptures, come clear as Wayne presents them in relevant form, all while humbly giving the credit and glory to God and God alone. Wayne's heart can be captured in one of his favorite verses, Psalm 27:4, "One thing I ask of the LORD, this is what I seek: that I may dwell in the house of the LORD all the days of my life, to gaze upon the beauty of the LORD and to seek Him in his temple."

Mark Vermeer, vice president of Katelyn's Fund,
Senior Ag/Business Banker Officer at People's Bank

CONTENTS

FOREWORD

W hat an honor to write this foreword and to invite you to jump into this book, to see the heart of my dear friend, who has taught me so much and been an example to follow after, and ultimately to see our Father's heart to follow. Wayne is truly is one of the kindest people I know, who loves deeply and gives generously of His time. He carries a confidence, not in himself, but a Holy Spirit confidence. Wayne is smart, very smart, and could be intimidatingly so, but his presence is just the opposite, so approachable, so very kind, that others are drawn to him. You feel like you want to just sit and soak up time with him. He is so filled with the joy of the Lord, and his smile lights up a room. We have shared many times in crazy laughter, leaving us in tears, and many times in tears, grappling with how such hard things will ever see joy.

As you read this book, find a comfortable place to settle in, allow yourself to take time to fully absorb it, like you are with a good friend, listening closely, and not feeling rushed. You will want to take time, as there is much to take in; after all, it is an invitation. Give yourself space to read and perhaps reread things. This book is for those wondering about who the Lord is, and for those wondering, if there is more to knowing Him. We each wear a different pair of glasses, with lenses that shape our perceptions and through which we look to gather and see the truth. The glasses we wear matter, and how we look at things makes a difference. Wayne is one with kingdom vision, one who seeks and strives to lean into and live a Psalm 27 life. One of his favorite verses is Psalm 27:4, "One thing I ask from the Lord, this only do I seek: that I may dwell in the house of the Lord all the days of my life, to gaze on the beauty of the Lord and to seek Him in His temple." It is rooted in a deep desire to know the Father's heart and to make that the place to give time and affection, a striving to find Him, looking for *the entrance* into the holy place with Him. What we seek after and what we give our time to, ultimately reveals what we love and what our heart's affections reflect. It is not about arriving but about striving. We will always have more to learn, ways to grow, and opportunities to deepen our faith.

Wayne is a wise man and diligent student, one who has spent hours studying the Word, pondering it, reflecting on it, analyzing it, and looking for confirmation in it as a place to stand on. As a former teacher, he understands the importance of studying to learn the content but also becomes personally knowledgeable about it for yourself. The Lord has imparted this desire to Wayne through the prompting of the Holy Spirit and wisdom through many decades of study. Wayne walks in deep humility and continues to carry a teachable heart. If you were in a face-to-face conversation with him, you would get a glimpse into the kindness that he walks in, given from the Lord, and a reflection of our Father. As you read this book, you will be moved by Wayne's testimony, by the power of the Father's mercy, love, and transformation. I believe He will show that this same mercy, love, and transformation is for each one who reads this, that your story is known to Him, and His love is for you.

The Father has given Wayne a shepherding heart, one that cares for others well and loves deeply, just as our Father does. He has a pierced heart for the Lord and a burden to share with you how you too can know Him and walk in freedom, whatever your journey has been and no matter what your view of the Father looks like through the lenses you have right now. As we have served in ministry together a long time, I have been able to observe not only Wayne's deep desire to know and lean into the Father's heart but his sincere desire for others to do the same. Over and over, we have discussed how it is not enough to *know about Him* but the need to *really know Him.* The opportunity this book offers is a way to do just that, to come as one striving to find Him *for yourself.* This invitation to intimacy is for you. Choosing Jesus is the biggest decision of your life. Allowing yourself to surrender everything over to Him will give you the fullness of life you seek, that place of belonging that is eternal, and He will overwhelm you with abundant life. Not that all things will be perfect, but He will flood you with His presence and peace. So those that are wondering, you are in the right place, so allow yourself time to really lean in to listen. Those that are seeking, keep looking, allow yourself time to learn on your own. Finally, those that are longing take courage. He sees you; therefore, allow yourself the freedom to experience all that He already sees for you and invites you to. Reluctant heart, let it sink in and let go. Resistant heart, give in; it will be worth it. Rescued heart, be at peace, and rejoice.

Trust that as you open up this book and take time to dig into it, you will be blessed, and you will be challenged. It's an invitation for you. Don't miss it or all that He has for you. You will be able to look into the Father's heart and to sit with Him, to see He is approachable and so very kind, and that He gives joy, holding you when there are many tears. He knows you and invites you to really come in close and seek to know Him fully.

Sheila De Jong
Founder and President
Katelyn's Fund Orphan Ministry

Introduction

One of the most significant needs in the church today is to know God intimately. We have some knowledge about God but need to know God, which is vastly different. We know some of the facts about God but often do not know Him personally, not possessing a living faith in the heart. We have a moderate understanding of what we should do and should not do. We assume to know what is required to just "get by," but we do not know without a doubt that we are walking with the Lord. We have been assuming all is good without the knowledge of what the scriptures teach. How do we arrive at such confidence, knowing for sure salvation is certain? Perhaps the more significant question is, where and how does such a desire originate?

There is much good material available on the Christian life and what our lives should look like, but we often are left wondering: how do I get to that point? We need to ask what is lacking in our knowledge and in the teachings we received, or maybe in our understanding of what we thought we heard. Why do so many laypeople have so many questions over the assurance of salvation and other critical issues?

My awakening happened when I didn't even know what was lacking in my life. Many people, churched and unchurched, are unaware of their need for a deep relationship with the Lord. The biblical way of satisfying that deep hunger in the soul is unknown. I attended church from the time of conception until now. A few weeks after I was born, without my knowledge, I was later informed that I was baptized. As I grew, I learned all the Bible stories at home and in church, memorized the catechism, and joined our church. In the process, I made many assumptions about God and salvation. I was operating on a religious level rather than a spiritual level—the difference being, where I would spend eternity.

I sense a great hunger within the laity (not ordained as pastors) for material providing answers to numerous questions. Through the help of the Holy Spirit, God has graciously provided me with many answers. The Holy Spirit has given me a burden for the kingdom and other laypeople having such struggles. Over the centuries, the church has drifted far from New Testament initiation into the kingdom of God. There is a God-given realization in the church of a significant need for the fullness of the gospel. There are too many loopholes in our understanding of the gospel and too many omissions in our numerous, so-called theologies.

Adequate knowledge of the Holy Spirit is a high priority as a higher number of Christians testify to the working of the Spirit in their lives. The fullness of the Spirit will be a necessity to survive the coming persecution preceding the second coming of Jesus, which will be greater than anything humanity has yet experienced (Matt. 24:21). It will require the one Spirit to transform the bride into the one body unifying the one body before Jesus returns. The move of the Spirit, creating a deep relationship with the Lord will be necessary well before Jesus's return, not just when it gets close. Matthew 25 explains that when Jesus is at the door, some will have oil in their lamps, and others will not. Also, millions will be completely unprepared. Jesus will return when least expected, like a thief in the night (Matt. 24:43).

The questions and lack of knowledge among the laity are concerning. The laity assumes they heard it all while attending church, and no additional study is needed. Often, the feeling among the laity is that they are not capable of studying and understanding scripture. They feel only pastors with seminary training are trustworthy, and that pastors are the only ones who are permitted to interpret and teach scripture because they have been ordained as "ministers of word and sacrament." Such thoughts are familiar with congregants. Therefore, laypeople disqualify themselves from studying scripture.

I am convinced that any literate person having a proper translation of the Bible is capable of reading the Bible with adequate understanding. It is not necessary to have a seminary degree to profit from studying the Word of God; even children can gain much from a Story Bible or a translation like the New Living Translation. Pastors can help much in clarifying the meaning of words that may mean something different in the original language or for which there is not an adequate word in our language. Also, information on cultural differences may be necessary for a clear understanding. Pastors are to enrich our study by providing a deeper understanding.

But, the primary reason for biblical illiteracy is the lack of a living relationship with the Lord, which produces hunger for His Word. If we do not have such an appetite, we need to examine our relationship with God seriously. My story has caused many to ask questions concerning their experience with the Lord. The uncomfortable part is that I went to church all my life and was not saved. There are many sitting in the pew on Sundays purely out of habit, falsely thinking all is well. Unfortunately, many are never exposed to the truth concerning salvation. There is a great need for truth.

ABOUT THE AUTHOR

After sharing my testimony with many different groups, especially youth groups, I was encouraged and felt inspired to write my story. As a high school math teacher, I led the local Youth for Christ chapter during my last seven years of teaching. That experience brought me into an awareness of the uncertainties and challenges our youth continually face. After retiring from teaching, I worked on staff in our church for almost seven years as director of calling ministry, which provided an awareness of the most significant concerns of many adults, and especially those near the end of life.

At the top of the list in every camp, the question most often asked is, how do I know for sure I am saved? Others are, how does salvation happen? What does a person experience, if anything, when coming to Christ? What changes will take place in my life? What effect will this have on friendships? Is God mad at me? What does the Holy Spirit living in you mean? And many other questions are on people's minds. Answers to these questions are critical to those asking.

The Holy Spirit has been prompting me to write a book, not only to share my story, but to use scripture explaining what and how the Holy Spirit worked in my life to bring about my transformation. I will show the pattern of the foundation taught in the New Testament concerning apostolic initiation into the kingdom of God.

Some years back, my daughter, Susan, gave my wife, Fran, and myself each a book at Christmas time, which requested recording significant events in our lives from as far back as one can recall, and then the books are to be returned as a legacy. That request was another confirmation to me that I needed to be obedient to the Spirit and record the working of the Holy Spirit in my life. The contents are what I strongly desire for my children, grandchildren, any future descendants, and friends to know. I feel a calling to share my story and leave the results or consequences of His calling up to the Spirit. I simply need to be obedient in writing my story.

I want to be upfront in stating that I do not have a degree in theology, for which I am grateful. I have witnessed real blindness to the truth when a given set of lenses is placed on people as to how they are to view scripture. The Bible is clear that is the work of the Holy Spirit. Spiritual formation happens through proper spiritual disciplines. The Bible is clear and understandable, but it must be read carefully in its entirety. I did attend Sioux Falls Seminary to complete a course in Clinical Pastoral Education (CPE) to help equip myself for the calling ministry. All people in the classes were ordained pastors except for me. Such studies provided no theological training but were an excellent opportunity to rub shoulders with people from many religious backgrounds, offering insight into the many different lenses used to influence people's thinking and views on scripture.

My education is in the field of mathematics. Mathematical proof at the graduate level is taken to a whole new level over undergraduate work using the laws of logic, and so forth. Without going into detail, the skills used in strict mathematical proof are very beneficial in studying scripture. A vital concept in reasoning is that given the right set of assumptions, you can prove anything you like. Whenever you begin a new mathematical system with a different set of assumptions, you come up with a new set of conclusions, a new system. Likewise, in spiritual formation, every time we form another set of assumptions, we create another box into which we can place people, which is what happens in philosophy and, unfortunately, in theological studies as well. That is how we make so many denominations.

I am convinced that we have a much more significant reading problem in the church than a theology problem. We make assumptions to suit our liking, which is not entirely biblical, just a little different, and we end up with different systems of theology. How else would we come up with thousands of denominations? It has been my observation that scripture is often read carelessly and interpreted to fit a given theological system. Frequently, assumptions are made to arrive at conclusions agreeing with our experiences.

Remember, beginning with a different set of assumptions, you arrive at different conclusions. That is how we can make the Bible say whatever we want. When doing mathematical proof at the graduate level, one is required to read with precise interpretation and then proceed with strict reasoning, a necessity to arrive at the truth. I accept nothing less in the study of scripture, where truth is of eternal importance. I also believe anyone can read with precision and accuracy, provided you read carefully and frequently, allowing the Holy Spirit to speak to you. Each of us is personally responsible for discovering the truth.

As a layperson, the Holy Spirit has given me a deep passion for the laity. The questions and lack of knowledge among the laity are concerning. This lack borders on illiteracy. If one sits in the pew twice a Sunday for fifty Sundays a year, at thirty minutes per sermon, you have only fifty hours of messages, most of which are quickly forgotten due to the style of instruction. That does not come close to providing the knowledge of God; at best, it provides a little information about God. The laity, on the average, knows little about the scripture and feels little need to know. Many think, I'll trust my pastor since he is theologically educated; I have been taught in church assuming my denomination is pretty good. My pastor has convinced me I'm going to heaven when I die. There is a vast misconception that everything is okay, thinking, "When I die, I'm on my way to heaven, or at least I'm hoping so."

Despite the many sitting in church most of their lives, parishioners cannot offer a biblical reason for the assurance of salvation. Why is this? The laity has gotten so accustomed to allowing others, such as the pastors, to do all the studying, and they merely need to soak it in. As an educator, I know that only listening has the lowest retention rate of any method of instruction. Such practices of merely soaking it in result in biblical illiteracy. Each one must personally study their Bibles, allowing God's Word to penetrate your soul.

About the Book

I desire to write a book that is easily understood without all the theological jargon, although I will address a few teachings that seriously mess up the laity. In arriving at truth, it is essential to take off all denominational lenses and put on lenses given by the Holy Spirit. When God saved me, the Spirit gave me a deep desire for God's Word and truth—to study God's Word for myself. I discovered many things that I always assumed were scriptural but were not. I also found that it is a difficult thing to unlearn what I had always believed over extended periods to be the right teaching. The Holy Spirit is to be our teacher, and we do not need to be taught by people who have been influenced by wrong teaching. We need to discern the truth personally through the witness of the Holy Spirit.

> But you have received the Holy Spirit, and he lives within you, so you don't need anyone to teach you what is true. For the Spirit teaches you everything you need to know, and what he teaches is true—it is not a lie. (1 John 2:27; NLT)

> When the Spirit of truth comes, he will guide you into all truth. He will not speak on his own but will

tell you what he has heard. He will tell you about the future. (John 16:13; NLT)

The Holy Spirit, provided He indwells us, will lead and guide us into all truth. The Bible states that God is the truth, Jesus is the truth, the Holy Spirit is the Spirit of truth, and the Word of God is the truth. I do not want this book to be my opinion or the opinion of a denomination. Therefore, I will use much scripture. This verse is my standard in teaching and writing. My judgment will be stricter as a teacher.

"My brethren, let not many of you become teachers, knowing that we shall receive a stricter judgment" (James 3:1 NKJV).

In Matthew 23, there are many woes listed for religious teachers. All teachers must read this chapter because of the eternal consequences for both the teachers and hearers. Warnings of false teaching are prominent throughout the Bible. If false teaching were a concern at the time of the apostles, it certainly would be a serious matter after many centuries of man's interpretations.

Discerning Truth

We should not believe teaching if we cannot find it in the Bible. We are personally responsible for the study of scripture. We should not believe any preacher, teacher, or author if we cannot find it in the Bible, including this book. I am very aware of teachers using proof texts, and therefore, it will sound biblically correct when it is taken out of context, not aligning it with all of scripture and producing false teachings. Remember, Satan appears as an angel of light using false teachers.

For such are false apostles, deceitful workers, transforming themselves into apostles of Christ. And no wonder! For Satan himself transforms himself into an angel of light. Therefore it is no great thing if his ministers also transform themselves into ministers of righteousness, whose end will be according to their works. (2 Cor. 11:13–14; NIV)

There is a great deal of false and inadequate teaching out there. We need to be able to discern if education is true or false. We need to know the Bible that well. That is why lay people need to study the Bible for themselves. I do not mean merely reading but explore scripture by taking notes and praying for the Holy Spirit to show the truth. I always made lists on the cover pages of my Bibles of verses that speak to a particular topic. Baptism was one example. Every time I ran into a verse about baptism, I would write it on my list in the front or back pages of my Bible. I did this with many topics, which helped me to discern the truth. I wanted to study all the scripture on an issue because I desired the truth.

Make sure you read words carefully. Many do not distinguish between simple words like "and" and "or." "And" means both parts of the conjunction must be true while "or" means one or both are true, provided it is the inclusive "or." There is also an exclusive "or," which means only one of the two is right and is used very little. Read prepositions carefully. Watch for conditionals, statements that say if a given condition is met, then a particular conclusion follows. Some promises are not conditional, while many are conditional. Not all conditionals are stated explicitly in the "if … then …" form. For example: "those who are faithful to the end will be saved" is not in that form, but it can be restated in the "if … then …" format, as "if you are faithful to the end, then you will be saved." Notice the condition required is that "you are faithful to the end," and the conclusion is, "then you will be saved." These are just a couple of examples. Read slowly and precisely to arrive at the truth.

Another essential thing to remember when reading scripture is that you are attempting to gain more than head knowledge. Read scripture to get to know God better, discovering His emotions and feelings, such as His love and compassion for you. Your resulting response to the gospel will be one of love and gratitude for His incredible grace. Studying scripture like that will produce great joy and desire for more of Him. The head knowledge will be a consequence of your heart knowledge. Your primary goal is to know and love Him intimately.

I desire that scripture will draw you into a deep, intimate relationship with the Lord. This book will cover the primary teachings to give a proper start into a deep, personal relationship with Jesus through the Holy Spirit. This book intends to cover the fundamental issues of entering the kingdom as given in the Bible, without any of man's interpretations, additions, or subtractions. The Bible does not need any human-made help. It says what it means and means what it says.

With all scripture included, this book can become a handy tool for personal use, understanding, and proper initiation into the kingdom. It can be used to assist you in leading others to faith, providing a solid foundation on which the person can stand and become a disciple, accessing the power of God. This book can be purchased in bulk to give to others in blessing them and enriching their lives. It is designed to equip people in witnessing to those far from Jesus. The inclusion of scripture will make it more useable in small group discussions or classes as well. If desired, each chapter can be an independent topic. The book will hopefully equip the reader in ministering to others in the market place, in the workplace, in your backyard, in your garage, in your kitchen or living room. The topics covered are those Jesus and the apostles taught in scripture, laying the proper foundation for entrance into the kingdom and becoming a disciple of Jesus.

Profits from Book Sales

All profits from purchasing this book will go to Katelyn's Fund Orphan Ministry. The preface of this book is written by Sheila De Jong, founder and president of the ministry. You can check out the organization on the website, katelynsfund.org, which I suggest. All volunteers operate the organization, and 100 percent of funds go to ministry.

The origin of Katelyn's Fund is a very touching story that shows how God, in His sovereignty, turns heartbreak into kingdom advancement. The growth of Katelyn's fund has been impressive, showing God's favor and His love for the orphan. The organization awards grants in helping families adopt children, domestic and foreign, into a forever family and offers support to foster families. The organization is also rebuilding and supports an orphanage in Haiti destroyed in the earthquake of 2010. James 1:27 reads, "Religion that God our Father accepts as pure and faultless is this; to look after orphans and widows in their distress and to keep oneself from being polluted by the world."

I find it amazing how often God mentions the orphan in scripture, especially in the Old Testament. Justice is significant in God's heart as He has such compassion for the oppressed and downtrodden that it will be a judgment day issue. As we do unto others is what we do to God.

"The King will reply, "Truly I tell you, whatever you did for one of the least of these brothers and sisters of mines, you did for me" (Matt. 25:40; NIV).

Indeed, children who are unborn and are orphans are the least of "the least of these." Adoption is a perfect picture of the gospel. God adopts anyone, as His child, who is willing to come and receive Him.

CHAPTER 1

GOD ON THE MOVE

**"I am going to do something in your days that you would
never believe, even if someone told you."
(Acts 13:41; NIV [quoting Hab. 1:5])**

T he church is facing a head-on collision with the most significant event in its history: the return of Jesus. The church,
as a whole, has little awareness, and in many cases, no knowledge of this significant event. In many churches, there is little, if
any, teaching and preparation on the second coming. Much of the
learning that does take place is not in agreement with scripture. A
large segment of the organized church is falling away from God,
becoming much more liberal, rather than moving closer to God.
As the church is rapidly growing more liberal, it rejects the teachings of the New Testament.

At the same time, God is on the move, preparing a bride for
His Son, Jesus. He desires only the best for His Son, nothing less.
He wants a bride hot on fire for His Son, not even a lukewarm
bride (Rev. 3:15, 16). After all, what loving, caring father would
desire a cold or lukewarm bride for his son? Be assured God the
Father will never allow that for His beloved, one and only Son

in whom the Father is well pleased. Indeed, the heavenly Father desires nothing but the best for His Son, Jesus!

His bride will be entirely in love with Him, anxious for His return, and in hot pursuit to know Him more intimately. The most important question will be: have you fallen in love with Jesus? Is He your first love? Sadly, many have not yet experienced a deep first love and still need a genuine encounter with Jesus through the work of the Holy Spirit. And, if you have had an actual encounter with Jesus and have lost that first love, you need to repent of no longer being intimately in love with Jesus, "or else your lampstand will be removed." Your lampstand is your church as a light, or witness to a broken world.

> But I have this complaint against you. You don't love me or each other as you did at first! Look how far you have fallen! Turn back to me and do the works you did at first. If you don't repent, I will come and remove your lampstand from its place among the churches. Anyone with ears to hear must listen to the Spirit and understand what he is saying to the churches. To everyone who is victorious, I will give fruit from the tree of life in the paradise of God. (Rev. 2:4, 5, 7; NLT)

He who has a spiritual ear must listen to what the Spirit is saying, or he will not eat from the tree of life in the paradise of God. This is a sober warning. Do you possess a love that is red hot for Jesus? Jesus is coming back for all those who love His appearing.

> So Christ was offered once for all time as a sacrifice to take away the sins of many people. He will

come again, not to deal with our sins, but to bring salvation to all who are *eagerly* waiting for him. (Heb. 9:28; NLT, my emphasis)

And the prize is not just for me but for all who *eagerly* look forward to his appearing. (2 Tim. 4:8; NLT, my emphasis)

Note the word *eagerly* in both verses. These verses beg the question: how can we love His appearing without knowledge of our bridegroom's return? If we are eager to meet Him, wouldn't we desire to know the details, like how, where, what will it be like, how can I prepare, and so on? We certainly would with a person we loved deeply and were eager to see.

Be assured the powers of darkness are acutely aware of the return of Jesus and their coming doom; consequently, they are out to deceive as many as possible. Deception has been taking place since the beginning of humanity. It was prevalent during the writing of scripture and has continued throughout church history. Little by little, some teachings are modified into false teachings, paralyzing the church. Some instructions have been entirely dismissed and never recovered. There is so much more to the gospel than we often realize. If we would only read scripture for ourselves, life would be so much more abundant. The church has allowed men to be their teachers, honoring them as great theologians, rather than having the Holy Spirit as their only teacher through God's Word.

"But you have received the Holy Spirit, and he lives within you, so you don't need anyone to teach you what is true. For the Spirit teaches you everything

you need to know, and what he teaches is true—it
is not a lie" (1 John 2:27; NLT).

Satan, with all the powers of darkness, is busy promoting lies
and deception, which is the origin of all false teaching. The forces
of darkness have encouraged denominations to overreact toward
one another, distorting the truth. Bible prophecy is a hindrance
to Satan's work, and therefore, he has created much doubt concerning prophecy. For centuries, prophecy has been made light of
and put down with many false teachings. Some say that prophecy
cannot be interpreted literally and, therefore, is explained away
by unbiblical teachings. For example, there is a teaching that the
church has replaced Israel, and consequently, the many prophecies concerning Israel are claimed to no longer be valid. They are
reapplied to the church, eliminating and subtracting much scripture—there are many informative prophecies concerning Israel
that reveal the greatness of God. The work of Satan is to conceal
the power of God.

There exist teachings that remove parts of the book of
Revelation, like the thousand-year earthly reign of Christ with all
the saints. Scripture commands us not to remove any words from
this book of prophecy, or our share in the tree of life will be taken
away, which is Satan's desire. This is a grave error! The Word of
God clearly warns us: "And if anyone removes any of the words
from this book of prophecy, God will remove that person's share
in the tree of life and in the holy city that is described in this book"
(Rev. 22:19 NLT).

Some also distort the meaning to say something different from
what it means. Many excuses have been made throughout church
history to do away with or to water down prophecy. Some felt that
these events were impossible, and it did appear that way many
years ago. But, today, we no longer have such excuses since we

can see the possibility of a literal fulfillment of events, such as the mark of the beast, which is now literally possible. Some prophecy is sealed for understanding until the time of the end (Dan. 12:9). But all prophecy will be fulfilled. God's Word is trustworthy and dependable.

There exists teaching that not only prophecy but the other gifts of the Holy Spirit are no longer functioning. Satan hates the work of the Holy Spirit that cripples his efforts and overcomes his power in spiritual warfare. Satan wants us to be powerless and ineffective, so that he has a much more significant influence in the world. Satan's desire is for us to be as ignorant as possible of the working of the Holy Spirit and has been instigating and refining his lies throughout history. Before the return of Jesus, there will be an incredible outpouring of the Holy Spirit, resulting in a great revival with an abundant harvest. "This gospel of the kingdom will be preached in the whole world as a testimony to all nations, and then the end will come" (Matt. 24:14; NIV).

Satan wants us to believe there is no such thing as the baptism in the Holy Spirit after coming to faith or that it was automatic; therefore, you need to do nothing to receive it. He wants us to believe that the gifts of the Holy Spirit ceased after the writing of scripture. Without the Holy Spirit's power, we are defenseless in spiritual warfare, which would be to Satan's advantage. The kingdom of God will not advance without the work of the Holy Spirit. Satan fears this power as much as anything and will do anything to stop it. The fullness of the Holy Spirit is and will be essential to survive spiritually in the end times, which Satan knows full well.

All the gifts of the Holy Spirit, such as the gift of discernment, will be essential to avoid the many deceptions which will seem to be the truth but will originate from the Father of lies. All the gifts of the Holy Spirit will be crucial and in full operation during this time, which will be very offensive to many. God loves us so much that He will pour out His Spirit in unprecedented ways in the end times. "And afterward, I will pour out my Spirit on all people. Your sons and daughters will prophesy, your old men will dream dreams; your young men will see visions. Even on my servants, both men and women, I will pour out my Spirit in those days" (Joel 2:28–31; NIV).

Peter preached part of Joel's prophecy at Pentecost, and Jesus used part of the same prediction in explaining the end-time events. Other prophecies indicate a revival like never before with a great harvest from every tribe, nation, and tongue, accompanied by great persecution before Jesus's return. *Jesus said,* "Then you will be handed over to be persecuted and put to death, and you will be hated by all nations because of me" (Matt. 24:9; NIV).

Are we prepared for such a move of God, pouring out His Spirit, causing Satan to pour out persecution like never before experienced by anyone? Since we do not know the day or the hour, preparation is necessary for He will come at an hour we do not expect (Matt. 24:44).

The end-time battle will be over *truth*. This great battle will take place in the heavenly realms as well as on the earth. God the Father is the *truth*; Jesus is the way, the *truth*, and the life; and the Holy Spirit is the Spirit of *truth*. Therefore, the Word of God is the *truth*. There will be a great deception and much false and confusing teaching before Christ returns as Jesus warns. Jesus said, "At that time many will turn away from the faith and will betray and hate each other, and many false prophets will appear and deceive many people" (Matt. 24:10,11; NIV). Additionally, false prophets will perform great signs and miracles deceiving many: "For false Messiahs and false prophets will appear and perform great signs and wonders to deceive, if possible, even the elect" (Matt. 24:24; NIV).

Both followers of Jesus and evil forces will possess mighty power to perform miracles on that day. Will you be able to discern the difference between real and false prophets, both performing such miracles on that day? Who will you trust or believe? Christians will need to be well-grounded in the Word of God or perish. Many teachers have never studied scripture for themselves and, consequently, teach as they have been taught, whether right or wrong. We need to study the Bible, not just read it. We must examine the Bible for ourselves, allowing the Holy Spirit to be our teacher. The church desperately needs to go deep with God, into the knowledge of God, not just learning about God.

It should be evident that the father of lies is behind deception through false teachings. We can blame deception on our churches, pastors, seminaries, but the enemy is the deceiver. Ultimately, we are personally responsible for knowing the truth. We have the gift of His Word. Before the printed Word came into existence, we may have gotten by with such blame, but today we have the written Word in many versions and have no excuse. We have been given much, and much will be required. We are personally responsible for our study of the Word. As laypeople, we need to study the Word for ourselves, relying on the Holy Spirit to be our teacher. The scriptures contain many warnings concerning false teachers and false teaching. Will you be able to recognize falsehood?

Satan fears the second coming because his doom is sure, and his destructive work will end. We can see why he does not want the church to know about specific end-time events that must take place. He hates the church and wants to destroy it, taking as many as possible to hell with him. "The thief comes to steal, and kill, and destroy; Jesus comes to give life and have it to the full" (John 10:10; NIV).

One of the purposes of prophecy is to prepare us with knowledge, protecting us, and to provide strength and encouragement in being faithful to the end (Matt. 24:13). We need to be prepared to be courageous and loyal even though the most vigorous persecution imaginable takes place as prophesied in scripture. Jesus gives a strong warning concerning persecution that will immediately occur before He returns (Matt. 24:21). Are you prepared for such testing?

The bride of Christ will be a worshipping church. It will be much different than "traditional worship." It will be all out, expressive worship. It will be heartfelt worship, "in spirit and truth." It will go forth from a heart full of love for Jesus. The beauty of the Lord will overcome the bride. David, when accused of worshiping God too exuberantly, said: "I will become even more undignified than this" (2 Sam. 6:22; NIV). The bride will be worshippers after God's own heart. The gifts of the Spirit will flow in worship as in 1 Corinthians 14. Today such worship would be offensive and would be met with persecution and even removal from the church.

"All this I have told you so that you will not fall away. They will put you out to the synagogue; in fact, the time is coming when anyone who kills you will think they are offering a service to God. They will do such things because they have not known the Father or me" (John 16:1–3; NIV).

The true bride of Christ will be so in love with Jesus that nothing else will matter. They will be willing to die for Jesus. Revelation 12:11 (NIV) states, "They did not love their lives so much as to shrink from death." There will be a time of incredible persecution, the greatest in all of history. Is the church ready? Are you ready? Who will prepare the church?

"For then there will be a time of great distress, unequaled from the beginning of the world until now—and never to be equaled again" (Matt. 24:21; NIV).

How do we feel about such persecution? The apostles rejoiced because they had been counted worthy to suffer disgrace for the name of Jesus (Acts 5:41)! Can we say that? Persecution has often purified and unified the church making it holy. The Bible states that Jesus will "return for a radiant church without stain or wrinkle or any other blemish, but holy and blameless" (Eph. 5:27; NIV). What is the state of the church? Are we such a church, without spot or blemish? Are we without stain or wrinkle, holy and blameless? Are we radiant, portraying the glory of God?

The Bible also says that there is a great shaking coming to shake everything that can be shaken (Heb. 12:26, 27). We have thousands of denominations, each with something upon which disagreement rests. Each one claims the Latin phrase, *sola scriptura*, which means, beliefs based on scripture alone. Really? It is impossible to have many interpretations of the same scripture. We have many explanations with high-sounding arguments and philosophies of men. We identify ourselves with various denominations originating from different leaders. We claim to follow Luther, Calvin, the pope, Wesley, Edwards, and the list goes on and on. Paul calls following various leaders worldly (1 Cor. 3:1–9; NIV).

Jesus is not returning for such a divided bride, but a united bride. We must recognize and admit we have a lot of blemishes. We are to be of one mind keeping the unity of the Spirit through the bond of peace.

> I, therefore, the prisoner of the Lord, beseech you to walk worthy of the calling with which you were called, with all lowliness and gentleness, with longsuffering, bearing with one another in love, endeavoring to keep the unity of the Spirit in the bond of peace. There is one body and one Spirit, just as you were called in one hope of your calling. (Eph. 4:1–4; NKJV)

I am fully aware of the excuses and even the proclaimed benefits of having many theologies. The Bible says we are to be one, even in our minds and thoughts. "I appeal to you, brothers and sisters, in the name of our Lord Jesus Christ, that all of you agree with one another so that there may be no divisions among you and that you may be perfectly united in mind and thought" (1 Cor. 1:10; NIV)

There will be much shaking in the church in preparation for the return of the bridegroom, Jesus. Many are already asking what is going on in the church. Why all the changes, especially with the new worship music? Why are people raising their hands and doing all sorts of other weird things? Why do people agree in prayer out loud? Why the shouting and clapping? Why do we have drums and guitars? Why the long extended times of worship? Why so much repetition? It is not the way we used to do it. The bridegroom is returning for a bride that worships uninhibited and with all their heart, soul, mind, and strength.

The Father is on the move, beginning to pour out His Spirit, preparing a bride for Jesus. Nothing less than an on-fire bride will do for the King of kings and Lord of lords. Jesus is worthy of worshiping hearts! I love worshipping with young people who have a burning heart for the Lord, those who love to gaze upon the beauty of the Lord. Yes, there maybe some excesses but not nearly as many as there are deficiencies. Persecution will take care of any excesses if there are any. Look at the scene in heaven, showing real worship in Revelation 4 and 5; it is loud and extravagant. In Revelation 4:8, we observe repetitive worship day and night.

> In a loud voice they were saying: "Worthy is the Lamb, who was slain, to receive power and wealth and wisdom and strength and honor and glory and praise!" (Rev. 5:12; NIV)

> In heaven, the four living creatures keep saying
> day and night, "Holy, holy, holy is the Lord
> God Almighty, who was, and is, and is to come."
> (Rev. 4:8; NIV)

> Every creature in heaven and on earth and under
> the earth and on the sea, and all that is in them,
> saying: "To him who sits on the throne and to the
> Lamb be praise and honor and glory and power,
> forever and ever!" (Rev. 5:13; NIV)

We need to meditate on that kind of worship and pray for His will to be done on earth as it is in heaven.

These changes are only the beginning. There already exists much criticism by famous theologians, and such complaining will only increase. What will be said when Christians begin to worship according to 1 Corinthians 14? When God starts to pour out His Spirit, many will be offended, and the love of many will grow cold, resulting in extreme persecution. Jesus said:

> All this I have told you so that you will not fall
> away. They will put you out of the synagogue
> (places of worship); in fact, a time is coming when
> anyone who kills you will think he is offering a
> service to God. They will do such things because
> they have not known the Father or me. I have told
> you this, so that when the time comes, you will
> remember that I warned you. (John 16:1–4; NIV)

> Then you will be handed over to be persecuted and
> put to death, and you will be hated by all nations
> because of me. At that time, many will turn away

from the faith and will betray and hate each other, and many false prophets will appear and deceive many people. Because of the increase of wickedness, the love of most will grow cold, but the one who stands firm to the end will be saved. (Matt. 24:9–13; NIV)

Many will turn away from the faith because they do not have the proper knowledge. They will only have religious, traditional head knowledge and not a real heart knowledge of God the Father, Jesus, and the Holy Spirit. On average, the knowledge of God and who He is is minimal in the church today, a dangerous position as the day approaches. Everything that can be shaken will be shaken, including the lukewarm, apostate Church (Heb. 12:25–29). "Many will be purified, cleansed, and refined by these trials. But the wicked will continue in their wickedness, and none of them will understand. Only those who are wise will know what it means" (Dan. 12:10; NLT).

There is only one thing that will preserve you through the shaking ahead: intimacy with God, the Father; His Son, Jesus; and the Holy Spirit. The knowledge of all three will be mandatory to endure. The Bible says that only those who have extra oil, the oil of intimacy, for their lamps will be ready and prepared. As stated earlier, at the last minute, you will not be able to borrow oil from another. You will personally need oil for your lamp ahead of that time. Preparation ahead of time is a necessity. Read the story in Matthew 25:1–13 about the ten virgins or bridesmaids. Half of those who were considered virgins or bridesmaids were waiting for His return and yet did not enter. That is a sobering thought. But notice Jesus's reply to those who could not come: "Believe me, I don't *know you!*" (Matt. 25:12; NLT, my emphasis). When Jesus prayed in John 17, He also said: "And this is the way to have eternal life—to *know you*, the only true God, and Jesus Christ, the one you sent to earth" (John 17:3; NLT, my emphasis).

Notice both times He says to *know* Him. That is critical, and we will explore scripture to see just what that entails. How do we become part of the bride of Christ and survive? This book will show you the solid foundation necessary to follow Jesus effectively in the days ahead. It is the way taught by Jesus and the apostles in the New Testament, the basics for kingdom entrance. The loving provisions of Jesus need to be received in enabling us to endure to the end. God has prepared the way and is moving to bring about the greatest revival humanity has ever witnessed, and at the same time, the great apostasy will be going on.

Questions for discussion:

1. In what ways have you observed God on the move in the church?
2. In what ways have you observed Satan using people to resist God's leading?
3. What moves of God have made you uncomfortable?
4. Do you feel prepared for end-time events Jesus speaks of in Matthew 24?
5. Do you realize the difference between knowing about God and knowing God?
6. How do you feel about being in love with God?
7. Are you aware of any false teachings in the church?
8. How do you feel about enduring persecution?

CHAPTER 2

MY SALVATION TESTIMONY

ເ∕ᢙᡕᠵ

**"For it is with the heart that you believe and are justified,
and it is with the mouth that you confess and are saved"
(Rom. 10:10; NIV).**

F orty-nine years have passed since an encounter with Jesus
Christ through the power of the Holy Spirit that completely
changed my life. The Lord's plan for me originated before the
foundations of the earth and began on this earth on February 4,
1939. I was born on a small farm just outside of Sioux Center, a
small town in northwest Iowa, the firstborn of seven siblings. The
date of my birth in history is significant in that those times were
so different from now. There was no affluence like we see today.
The country was just coming out of the Great Depression, and
World War II was on the horizon, which began December 7, 1942,
creating high anxiety and concern.

At that time, we traveled in a Model A Ford. We milked cows
by hand and farmed with horses. We never heard of technology;
we did not have electricity when I was born. I remember the elec-
trician wiring our house and barn when we did get electricity. The
first tractor was an F-20 Farmall with 20 horsepower. As a small

child, I remember vividly, my dad's brother being killed in World War II and the great sorrow in my dad's family over his death.

A few years after my birth, we moved to another farm near Orange City, Iowa, where we lived until the spring of the year that I was in the eighth grade. At that time, my parents sold our dairy operation to make a down payment on a farm near Montevideo, Minnesota, where our family moved. I attended country school in Iowa and completed the eighth grade in a country school near our Minnesota farm place and went on to high school in Milan, Minnesota, where I graduated.

My parents grew up experiencing the Great Depression and therefore started with nothing and out of necessity were very conservative. We wasted nothing. Some feed for livestock was purchased in cloth sacks, and my mother used the material from the feed sacks to make shirts for the boys and dresses for the girls. We had the necessities but certainly nothing extra. We lived on the farm where we grew and raised much of our food, selling the rest to buy other necessary items. Life at home was often uncertain financially. With the selling down of our dairy operation and other livestock, the exception being a few head of animals and essential machinery, we were far from affluent. We started entirely over, rebuilding our livestock herds.

When I attended high school, there was not enough money to buy hot lunches, so I carried my lunch while my peers ate in the school cafeteria. Physically, I was the smallest one in my class until my senior year when I finally grew. I was far from an athlete and was often the last one picked to be on a team when choosing sides. Many times I acted out to gain some attention and hopefully avoid getting picked on by my peers. I had two sets of clothes so that while wearing one set, the other was in the wash. Life was filled with hard work on the farm, staying home from school for lengthy periods, weeks at a time to help with the farming, resulting in low achievement in school. There were other issues, and everything put together resulted in my significant feeling of inferiority and low self-esteem.

My dad was a hard worker, high strung, and had a quick temper, always keeping the level of concern high, never knowing when he might lose it. He had two personalities. In public, he was full of laughter, leading many to think that he was easygoing and lots of fun. He was an elder and a Sunday school teacher in our church. Usually, he was close to our pastors. He was very denominational in his thinking and was very serious about bringing up his family to fit into the same mold. He was very much in control and had rigid expectations for his children. If anyone did not live up to his expectations, the consequences would not be desirable. In today's society, his methods of discipline would be considered abusive. That word was not used in that day.

Personally, the physical punishment which I received was frequently extreme, and I could have tolerated that, but the words that accompanied such physical discipline were devastating. I repeatedly heard the words that I was worthless; I didn't amount to a hill of beans; I was nothing but a big disappointment and would never amount to anything. These remarks were often laced with profanity, having a profound effect on my formation.

On one incident, he said that I was such a disappointment that he didn't want me anymore. He proceeded to send me up the driveway and told me to leave. I would take a few steps out of fear of what would happen if I did not listen, and then I would stop because I was too afraid to leave, not knowing what would happen to me or where I would go if I did leave. When I would stop, he would yell at me to get going. The cycles of commands to get going and my stopping repeated until I got to the end of the driveway, which seemed about thirty yards long. I was a young boy, maybe in fourth grade, and out of fear, I was crying very hard. When I got to the end of the driveway, I looked both ways and didn't know which way to go. I remember the panic, thinking, which way do I go? Where will I go when darkness comes? Fear overwhelmed my entire being.

At that point, my mom saw what was taking place and opened the house door and shouted: "John, that's enough." Hearing my mom, Dad stopped yelling at me, and the whole ordeal ended. I only remember cautiously coming back down the driveway, fearful and very uncertain of what might happen. I have no idea what would have happened if Mom would not have seen it and ended it. The entire ordeal was so traumatic that I do not remember anything else that happened or how the rest of the evening went. I only remember the incredible fear and the deep hurt that I was so undesirable and no longer wanted by my dad. I always felt that I tried hard to please, but it seemed impossible. I often thought if this is Christianity, I don't want any part of it.

There was also considerable neglect of family needs, partly due to poverty. I was not taken to a dentist until I was in the ninth grade. I had a mouth full of rotten teeth by the time I did go. When the dentist examined me, several teeth were beyond repair, so he had to pull them, and he put fillings in most of the rest of my teeth. Later the dentist took my dad into his office; I thought to explain things. When we got home, I remember overhearing my dad telling my mother what happened. It was, without a doubt, a serious conversation between Dad and the dentist, including threats concerning neglect. The dentist made my dad agree to take each one of my siblings and me to the dentist annually from then on. There were other issues, such as failing my first basketball physical exam in my freshman year due to a long-standing hernia that went unrepaired since childhood. Overall, my life experiences through high school were emotionally destructive, living in much fear as I matured.

Mom was a strong woman, working very hard outside and inside the house. She was strong physically and emotionally, never visibly displaying sympathy for herself. Despite her strength, she had a soft, tender place in her heart. She was a godly woman, and I would often see her on her knees in prayer by the bed before retiring at night. Despite her love, I had very low self-esteem. Having gone through such trauma, I did begin to believe that I was worthless and never would amount to anything. It was like permanently seared into my mind with a hot iron.

Our family was very religious, attending church twice on Sunday and once during the week, even though it was over twenty-five miles, round trip. We had table devotions with both scripture and prayer three times a day without fail. As children, we always attended Sunday school and Catechism classes, learning all the Bible stories, memorizing scripture, and learning our central denominational doctrines. In this upbringing and at the age of sixteen, I felt in my heart that I should join our church. There was no doubt the feeling was a prompting from the Holy Spirit. But, I was unfamiliar with the Holy Spirit and did not know what the Spirit was up to in my life.

I had no understanding of the work of the Holy Spirit in drawing and calling me, as described in John, chapter six. Even though I felt the Holy Spirit calling me, I did not have the biblical knowledge of how to respond. I do recall asking God that if I ever did anything stupid, to bring me back to Him. To join church, I had to appear before the elders of the church and profess my faith in Jesus Christ. Therefore, I appeared before the elders, and as they asked me some questions, I remember replying with memorized answers from the Heidelberg Catechism, which I had recently learned. The elders seemed to be impressed, probably because they would have been hard-pressed to do the same. So I was received into what they called "the visible membership of the church and was admitted to the Lord's Table," allowing me to take communion.

Since I was "baptized" as a baby and made a profession of my faith, I thought I was "good to go," and somehow, I would automatically go to heaven someday. I had no understanding of the new birth, surrendering my life to Christ, committing to follow Jesus, and being in an intimate love relationship with Jesus. I heard all the Bible stories, including the story of Nicodemus, but being born again did not seem to fit into the picture for me because I assumed I was already in the kingdom, as I understood, what they called covenant theology. I misunderstood thinking that being born again was for someone outside of the church, living in severe sin, doing drugs or some other serious thing, and, therefore, not applicable to me.

Despite all the church attendance and much teaching, and I am sure it was all worthwhile, the emphasis seemed to be on right and wrong living, which was not bad teaching but very incomplete. At home, Dad's teaching was that God had a big book where He kept track of all our deeds. Every time we did something right, He would put a white mark in the book, and every time we did something wrong, He would make a black mark in His big book. Then on the judgment day, He would count up the number of black marks and white marks. If you had more white marks than black marks, you would go to heaven. And if you had more black marks. you would go to hell. That was probably an incentive for a child to live obediently, but it is works-based teaching and wrong. We are saved by grace through faith and not of works (Eph. 2:8).

In our church, I never heard a salvation testimony from anyone, including a pastor, an elder, or a layperson like a Sunday school teacher. I never heard about anyone receiving Christ, having a personal relationship with Jesus, and what that meant. Nor did the elders ask me any questions like that when I made a so-called "profession of faith" The elders never questioned whether I had been personally born of the Holy Spirit. If you never hear, how can you believe it? The Bible says, "But how can they call on him to save them unless they believe in Him? And how can they believe in Him if they have never heard about Him? And how can they hear about Him unless someone tells them" (Romans 10:14; NLT).

I did hear one personal testimony when a group of young people from our church attended a Billy Graham Crusade in Minneapolis. That was from someone who was not brought up in a Christian environment, so again I figured that did not apply to me because I was brought up in a strict Christian home. I didn't need conversion since the pastor sprinkled me when I was a baby. I was declared to be a child of the covenant, predestined, one of His elect, and as I grew up, I acquired much knowledge about the Bible, God, and so forth since childhood. Surely that should get me into heaven.

After graduating from high school, and just turning seventeen, there seemed like no other choice but to work at home on the farm. I stayed home for a year and farmed with my dad. After about half of that year, I knew I did not want to farm with my dad for the rest of my life, nor was it healthy; I had to do something else and therefore began thinking about other options. Considering my interests, I started to feel like I needed to do something much different, which would require an education beyond high school. More education would be a challenge since I stayed home for weeks at a time to work while in high school; therefore, my achievement was meager, presenting a big problem. The importance of education was not stressed, nor did I develop an interest in school. I was interested in surviving.

Even though I was not a very good student in high school, I had a keen interest in designing new kinds of machinery and cars. I would often draw pictures of very sleek cars, thinking engineering would be exciting. I decided I needed to try college. After talking with my parents and receiving their approval, I decided to attend Northwestern College in Orange City, Iowa, near where I was born and lived as a child. It was a Christian college affiliated with my denomination, which felt comfortable. I did reasonably well in college and majored in mathematics, eventually becoming a math teacher. Socially, I had many friends in college and began to feel worth something. I completed my practice teaching in Sioux Center and spent my entire career teaching math in the Sioux Center Community School System.

After college graduation, my now-wife, Fran, and I got married and had two children, a girl and a boy, and we now have five grandchildren. Immediately, into my teaching career, I went on and received a master's degree in mathematics and did very well academically. I became a member of Lambda Sigma Tau, a national honorary society in mathematics and science. I gradually realized that I could and did amount to something, and it felt good.

After teaching in Sioux Center for ten years, a revival broke out in our high school. It all began when some of our high school boys attended a Fellowship of Christian Athletes camp, and while attending camp, they heard testimonies of professional athletes who gave their lives to Christ. Upon hearing powerful testimonies, they also gave their lives to the Lord. They came back fired up and vocal about their decision and new life in Christ. Our pastor heard the story and asked them to share their experience at a Sunday morning church service, an unheard-of occurrence in our church. We did not do testimonies and altar calls. They shared how their idols, the professional athletes, shared their testimonies of receiving Christ, and they were convicted and also decided to accept Christ into their lives.

These boys were brought up just like me, in a Christian home, and yet they were giving their lives to Christ, which was new to me. They testified to the new life and joy they experienced after coming to Christ. I never heard anything like that in church. The Holy Spirit was powerfully convicting me, tugging at my heart. Tears began flowing down my face. I was glad that I was sitting on the end of a row by the wall so that I could use my hand to cover the side of my face toward people, preventing others from seeing me weep. I was very accustomed to being hard and always having my emotions under control. I was embarrassed about all the tears, and at the same time, I started to realize my life needed a change. Like earlier in my life, I didn't know that the Holy Spirit was drawing me to the Lord.

Hearing four students testify was extremely powerful to me as a teacher. As a result of their testimonies and their witnessing, more students gave their lives to Christ, resulting in more testimonies in school. Every time another student shared their testimony, I experienced intense conviction from the Holy Spirit. I resisted as hard as I could, figuring that if I gave my life to Christ, I would lose my friends and life would no longer be fun. Considering all I had been through in my life, friends were significant, giving me a sense of belonging. Another reason I did not want to give my life to Christ was that I thought He would send me to Africa, and I didn't want to go there. It was like every power of darkness was working on me, attempting to prevent me from surrendering my life to Christ Jesus.

However, the Spirit did not give up and continued to draw me to Himself. One ordinary Sunday morning, as I was attending church, a group of people from our church returned from a missionary conference in Milwaukee. The power of the Holy Spirit was overwhelming. The pastor started the service by making a statement I will never forget. He said, "Today, something great is going to happen in this church." My body literally shook under the power of the Spirit; tears were flowing profusely. Near the end of the message, I prayed right where I was sitting, dead center, front row in the balcony, where I could not hide my many tears, I told God, "He could have me and my life." I said to God, "He could do whatever He wanted to do with me, that I was His from now on."

I didn't know the sinner's prayer or the four spiritual laws or any such thing, but in my heart, I fully surrendered my life to Him, and Jesus came right into my heart and life. What an incredible experience. It was like a huge burden was lifted from me, resulting in a feeling of freedom and joy like I had never experienced before in my life. It was like everything was different. I was a new person. I was full of joy. As I was leaving church driving home, I found myself doing a strange thing, praying for people I met, including one I did not like very well. Something drastic had happened in my life. I didn't know exactly what happened, but I was excited about it, and it felt good.

That same Sunday evening in my newfound excitement, I was singing in the choir at the evening service. During the service, I told God, "If there is an altar call, I will go forward, even if no else does" In a church where they did not give altar calls, there miraculously was one. Knowing God was doing something special at my request, I immediately jumped from my seat, came down from the choir loft to the front, not caring what anyone thought and unaware of anything going on around me.

A drastic change took place in my heart from being afraid of what others thought to not really caring, even hoping they might ask. After the prayer, I saw many others who came forward. Someone wisely told me to write the date in my Bible that I received Christ into my heart, which was October 10, 1971. That was good advice because now I can point to the exact time I was born anew. I was thirty-two years old at that time. Some statistics show that after age twenty-one very few people give their life to the Lord. Praise God the Holy Spirit is more powerful than any statistic. The work of the enemy and my resistance was no match for the power of the Holy Spirit.

The next day, Monday, was radically different at school. Word must have gotten around that Mr. Vermeer went forward at an altar call last night because a few students, with big smiles on their faces, commented that they were happy and excited about my decision. We had a pretty good-sized church of 1,000 people, and a lot of our students attended the same church I attended. Unbeknown to me, before surrendering my life to the Lord, a group of students confessed to me they were praying for me that God would intervene in my life. How amazing that the Holy Spirit inspired them to single me out and pray for me. Why single me out—why not another teacher? It was like God leaving the ninety-nine and going after the one that was lost. Amazing grace!

Many changes immediately took place in my life. My temper, which I effectively used for discipline in school, was gone. I had to come up with new ways to handle discipline, which in the end was far better for my students and me. The Monday night after my new birth, as I was in the process of building our house, I was installing siding around 10:00 p.m. with a 100-watt bulb hanging on the eve; I hit the wrong nail, my fingernail. I said, "Ouch," and began to laugh at the new and unusual response, which generally would have been a stream of profanity. My language from that time forward had changed entirely. But the most significant change of the many changes was an incredible desire and hunger for God's Word. I just wanted to know this Jesus who changed my life to the utmost. The Spirit placed a fierce love for Him within me. I had such a strong desire to know Him intimately, the one who forgave my many sins and changed my life so completely, bringing such joy in place of heaviness.

My entire life was changed. I did a one-eighty, surrendering myself to His will. I was no longer living for myself but living for Jesus. I asked forgiveness for all the sins I could think of at that time. The Holy Spirit revealed many more sins in my life as I continued to grow. I needed to make things right with some people I had mistreated. To some, I needed to apologize. To some, I had to make things right financially. I changed how I dealt with people and how I treated others personally. I repented as best as I knew how at that stage of the game. I didn't know some things I was doing were sins until the Holy Spirit revealed them to me. God was very gracious in showing me what changes needed to take place in my life in following Jesus. He is such a good Father.

In the revival taking place in our high school, many students would enter my classroom with their stack of books, the top book being their Bible. They would hurry to finish their homework, hoping there would be a little time left so that they could read in their Bibles. Now I was doing the same thing. I carried a small New Testament which fit in my shirt pocket, using it whenever I had a chance, even if I could only get a couple of verses to read. I couldn't wait to get into God's Word.

One of the boys in one of my classes, also very hungry for God's Word, asked me if I would meet with him to study our Bibles together during my preparation period, at which time he was in study hall. I agreed, and we would go down to the janitor's smoke room daily to study our Bibles until I got called into the superintendent's office about using that time for Bible study. The superintendent, with a smile on his face, said it would look better if I used that time as intended. I admitted that he was right, and I would use that time for preparation time and have Bible study at another time, which we did. We started an evening small group meeting on a weekly basis.

The revival was so powerful and contagious that many students gave their lives to the Lord. I recall a Sunday morning when one of my students went forward at the end of a sermon. There was not an altar call, but this young boy made his own altar call by just walking up front and kneeling. The pastor nearly lost it and was speechless for a moment. As the Spirit moves, the supernatural begins to happen. Not only did many students give their lives to the Lord, but many adults also did.

In my quest to know the Lord more intimately and in studying His Word, I realized why my love for Him was so all-consuming. The Holy Spirit had taken up residence in my heart, creating such hunger for God. Everything that changed was the work of the Holy Spirit. I had been so lost and didn't even realize it. I thought I was saved and on my way to heaven, but I was on the broad road of religion and headed toward destruction.

All those years in church and I didn't understand the gospel. My whole life changed. I lost my taste for alcohol, which had gotten way out of control, my language changed, my anger was gone, and I had the heart for people to receive Christ. But, the most significant change was Jesus living in my heart, creating a great hunger to know Him and His Word. I just wanted to know God more and more, not merely knowing about Him as I had in the past. All I could think about was Jesus. He became my first love. I wanted a deeper relationship with Him and desired to hear His voice, having fellowship with Him. I loved Him! Have you experienced a "first love" for Jesus?

Before my conversion, when I did read the Bible as a young person, my only option at the time was the King James Version of the Bible. This version was challenging, almost impossible, for me to understand because I didn't talk like that, and nobody I spoke with spoke like that. As I began supporting Billy Graham, he offered, and I requested a paperback copy of the Living Bible, which he sent. The Living Bible was so easy to read. Because of my intense hunger, and for the first time, the Holy Spirit was teaching me and leading me into truth, I learned more in the first year after my new birth with the Living Bible, than in the previous thirty-two years with all the religious teaching without Christ in my heart. At that point, the Living Bible was an excellent choice. It was so exciting to read with understanding. Shortly after that, someone gave me a copy of the New American Standard Bible, which was the hot translation with college students at that time. I began heavily studying the two versions side-by-side and thoroughly enjoyed them.

Immediately after surrendering my life to Christ, someone told me to read the gospel of John first. So I did, and I believe that was advice from the Spirit because, initially, without proper teaching, I did not fully understand what took place in my life. I only had to get to chapter 3 to discover the unbelievable change that had taken place in my life. I was born of the Holy Spirit, born again, born from above, born of God, all equivalent expressions of the same experience. Upon further study, I discovered so much more about what happens when you are born again, and everything I experienced was just like in scripture. I learned so much more by personally studying God's Word rather than listening to others preach and teach. When I researched the Word for myself and allowed the Holy Spirit to be my Teacher, rather than merely listening to others, was the time I found the truth.

Frequently, I hear people say, "All you have to do is believe in the Lord Jesus Christ, and you will be saved." But there is much meaning in the word *believe*. Believing in the Lord Jesus is far more than just thinking it in your head. James 2:19 says that even Satan believes that way and so much so that he lives in fear and trepidation. Believing includes repentance, inviting, and receiving Jesus into your heart, entering into a relationship that results in knowing the Lord, and then denying self and lovingly following Jesus in full obedience. The Bible gives many details in many places to what believing includes and means, but we must be willing to study and read for ourselves.

I learned that much of what I thought to be correct was false teaching. There were things I had to unlearn, which is far more complicated than learning something new. In allowing the Holy Spirit to be my teacher, the truth eventually prevailed. In addition to Bible study, I initially bought and read many books of testimony because every story was so exciting to read. Stories of people coming to faith were so affirming, encouraging, and faith-building. Testimonies defeat the power of darkness in lives.

After receiving Christ, I was invited to a Bible study group that met weekly at Central Café downtown, Sioux Center. There were a couple of other teachers and a bunch of different businessmen I knew in that group of at least a dozen men. Strangely, my fear of losing friends turned into having many more.

There are many other details in my conversion story. And I have many other testimonies in addition to my salvation testimony. I can give testimony concerning my healing from cancer, receiving the Holy Spirit as in scripture, the gifts, and fruit manifesting in my life, my baptism in water, the forgiveness of my dad, and other stories that will come up in later chapters.

My prayer for every reader is that the Holy Spirit will lead and guide each one into all truth. Truth does not depend on what I think, what any pastor thinks, or what any denomination thinks, but on what God says in His Word. Go hard after truth. Do not merely read but study God's Word. If you cannot find it in the Bible, do not receive it as truth. Depend on the Holy Spirit to be your teacher.

The Work of the Holy Spirit in My Salvation

It is critical to know what the scriptures say about being saved so that you are confident of your salvation. Being informed about being saved is also necessary knowledge in leading others to Christ when you witness, teach, preach, or mentor. The scriptures explain that rebirth is a work of the Holy Spirit. The Holy Spirit is a person and not an "it" The Holy Spirit is the third person of the Trinity. He is God, the Holy Spirit, and deserves our utmost respect.

When I heard the testimonies of my students, the Spirit was intense in pulling on my heart-strings. I tried to resist, as I explained in my testimony. Resisting worked for a while, and then the Spirit provided another testimony and then another, continuing one after another until I was fully convicted and convinced I needed Jesus in my life. Through the persistence of the Holy Spirit, the repetition continued until I could no longer resist the powerful drawing. Have you experienced the Holy Spirit tugging on your heart? If you have, that is the invitation to become one with Jesus. The working of the Holy Spirit is a necessary component of salvation, as I will explain in the next chapter.

The Spirit continues to perform His work to complete the initial process, convincing a person to surrender their life to Jesus. I also felt the Holy Spirit convicting me and encouraging me to repent of all of my sins He brought to my attention, and there were many. I have a problem with the apostle Paul saying he was the worst sinner ever born. I lived many years later. The load I carried was heavy, and the release through repenting and receiving forgiveness was huge. True repentance did not stop with only confessing to God, but to all, I had wronged.

After receiving Christ, our fallen nature is still there, as Paul explains in Romans 7. We need to die to that old nature we inherited, have it cut off in saying yes to Jesus, and we then need to bury it in water baptism (Rom. 6). When we first receive Jesus into our hearts, it may be easy to respond in love. But, we must remain in His love, and if we stray, we need to repent and return to our first love for Him as we read in Revelation 2:4–7. God loves us deeply and is jealous for our love. He wants us to love Him in return with our whole heart, soul, mind, and strength, that is, to love Him with our entire being. He will do whatever it takes to get our love. Are you in love with Jesus? So in love that you live, eat, and sleep, Jesus? Loving Jesus is the gate to the road we are to take, the narrow way, loving Jesus in full obedience to His teachings.

In the United States, we tend to make salvation very easy and cheap. We say all you need to do is pray a specific prayer, asking Jesus into your heart, and you have the assurance of going to heaven. Often, there is no mention of surrendering your life to Jesus, being delivered from sin, and then following Him in love and obedience to the very end. There indeed are those who have genuinely found Christ by saying a simple prayer when done sincerely and certainly when done with tears of conviction. But, many have never experienced the Holy Spirit working in their life and then responding to the call.

Some say the prayer for fire insurance, only hoping it will keep them from hell, which is not a full surrender, making Jesus Lord of life. Colossians 1:27 (NLT) states, "And this is the secret: Christ lives in you, and this is your assurance that you will share in his glory."

What matters, did Jesus get in your heart? Is He living in you? Do you sense His presence? If He is truly in your heart, you will want to live for Him. The next verse, 28, speaks of being in a *relationship* with Jesus, not merely knowing about Him. "So everywhere we go, we tell everyone about Christ. We warn them and teach them with all the wisdom God has given us, for we want to present them to God, *perfect in their relationship with Christ*" (my emphasis).

Many have experienced difficulty with my testimony simply because they do not understand the work of the Holy Spirit in the process of salvation. It has been hard for some to understand, being raised in the church and having attended your entire life, that one can still be lost. By attending church their whole life, they believe the default is heaven, but the default is hell because we are born in sin, and the only way out is through God's provision: Jesus Christ. I had a seminary professor question me, saying, "What do you mean you got saved when you have always been in church?" The Holy Spirit said, "He is another Nicodemus." How true.

Before salvation, I would say that I was saved because that is what I was taught. It was a religious conviction. I have also heard people say, "I prayed that prayer, so I know I'm saved." That is not a biblical reason for assurance of salvation. As you progress through this book, you will know what the Bible declares to be sure of salvation. It is so counter-cultural but straightforward.

It is essential to read the Bible for yourself, for many are led astray by false teaching and receive a false assurance of salvation. There are both inadequate and excessive teachings out there. In Matthew 16:5–12, Jesus warns about the teaching of religious leaders. In Matthew 16:11–12 (NLT), Jesus said, "Beware of the yeast of the Pharisees and Sadducees. Then, at last, they understood that he wasn't speaking about yeast or bread but the false teaching of the Pharisees and Sadducees (the religious leaders)." If we as laypeople do not read the Word for ourselves, we can quickly be led astray either by what we heard or by what we thought we understood. The Bible has loads to say about false teachers and false teaching. In times like these, we need to check out everything we hear. Know your Bible and the Lord.

It is so much more than just believing in our heads or having the correct set of "doctrines."

> Jesus said, "you can enter God's Kingdom only through the narrow gate. The highway to hell is broad, and its gate is wide for the many who choose the easy way. But the gateway to life is small, and the road is narrow, and only a few ever find it. ... Not all people who sound religious are godly. They may refer to me as Lord, but they won't enter the Kingdom of Heaven. The decisive issue is whether they **obey** my Father in heaven. On judgment day, many will tell me, Lord, Lord, we prophesied in your name and cast out demons in your name and performed many miracles in your name. But I will reply, I *never knew you*, go away; the things you did were unauthorized." (Matt. 7:13–14, 21–29; NLT, my emphasis)

Those are thought-provoking words. Reading carefully, we see that we need to *obey* God, and we need to *know* Him for our works to be authorized. We are under His authority. We need to submit to the jurisdiction He has in our lives and do everything to the honor and glory of God in love for Him.

Many, like me, assume since they were born in a Christian family, raised with Christian values, and have attended church since they were babies, that they are "good to go" and on their way to heaven. That is a lie. Jesus said, "You must be born again" In other words, there is no such thing as having been a Christian for all of your life. Being born again is also called being born of the Holy Spirit because it is entirely a working of the Holy Spirit. Being born again is also called being born of God, or born from above. The new birth does not happen when born of man. It is a supernatural birth, bought and paid for by everything Jesus did on the Cross for all who are willing to *receive*. It is a gift of grace, which must be received in faith. However, it is a gift that is of no value until received.

In the chapters following, we will examine in far greater detail what scripture has to say about the entire process of becoming a child of God. Jesus desires to save us because He loves us genuinely and wants us to be His children, sharing in the most beautiful inheritance imaginable. He has a beautiful plan for each one of us. Most people know John 3:16–17 (NLT): "For God so loved the world that he gave his only Son so that everyone who believes in him will not perish but have eternal life. God did not send his Son into the world to condemn it, but to save it."

We have a choice to remain in darkness or enter into the light. Each person is personally responsible for this choice. No one can choose for you. Paul says in Romans 9:2–3 (NIV), "My heart is filled with bitter sorrow and unending grief for my people, my Jewish brothers, and sisters. I would be willing to be forever cursed—cut off from Christ!—if that would save them." No one can receive salvation for you, no matter how much they desire it as Paul wanted for his brothers, but you must personally receive salvation. God's desire for each of us is to have a personal relationship with Him, and it would not be personal if someone else decided for us. We are called personally and need to respond personally. The beauty of the new covenant is that it is no longer just for a select few born into a specific lineage, but whosoever is willing may come. That is grace and the excellent way!

You cannot even become a Christian without the work of the Holy Spirit. In John 6:65 (NIV), Jesus makes it very clear, "It is the Spirit who gives eternal life. Human effort accomplishes nothing. And the words I have spoken to you are spirit and life."

Our effort cannot get us into heaven; the Spirit initiates salvation by drawing us to Jesus. How does that happen? It happens from hearing the Word of God. The Spirit draws powerfully through the Word of God. These words are "spirit and life" Other scriptures say the same thing. For example, Romans 10:17 (NLT) says, "Faith comes from listening to this message of good news—the Good News about Christ" Also, Ephesians 2:18 (NLT) says, "Now all of us, both Jew and Gentiles, may come to the Father through the same Holy Spirit because of what Christ has done for us."

The Holy Spirit worked powerfully in my heart, drawing me to Jesus through the testimonies of my students, and I responded by surrendering my life to Jesus, personally.

Jesus gives us this serious warning that only a few will find eternal life. Many will think they are saved and completely miss the boat. The entrance is very narrow, and many will not discover it. Satan is continually deceiving regular churchgoers with lies in their minds concerning the way to eternal life. Satan has been preparing his great deception throughout church history, preventing the truth from entering hearts. People like to look good on the outside while the inside is dead to the touch of the Spirit.

Questions for discussion:

1. Have you experienced a personal encounter with Jesus through the Holy Spirit?
2. Have you invited Jesus into your heart at some time? When?
3. Have you made a full surrender of your life to Jesus?
4. Can you share your story of salvation with others?
5. When and where have you shared your testimony?

CHAPTER 3

THE CALL

**"For many are called, but few are chosen"
(Matt. 22:14; NLT).**

I t is essential to have awareness of the working of the Holy
Spirit before salvation takes place. What has to happen in beginning the process of being saved? What does the Bible have to say
about being saved so that you can know for sure? The Holy Spirit
is wholly involved in every component of the salvation process.
Understanding the work of the Holy Spirit will increase our appreciation and gratitude for what Jesus accomplished on our behalf.
Such knowledge will enable you to have a much greater appreciation and love for the Holy Spirit. An in-depth understanding of
who the Holy Spirit is and what the Holy Spirit accomplishes in
our lives is essential to understanding salvation.

The Holy Spirit is God and has the same attributes as God the
Father and God the Son. The Holy Spirit loves us profoundly and
richly, and He, in turn, desires to be loved intimately as the Father
does. Holy Spirit blesses us with gifts and fruit. Holy Spirit is
all-powerful, all-knowing, and everywhere present with us always

and in all places. He is full of grace and truth. He is the Spirit of God and Jesus and, therefore, completely holy.

The Bible says He convicts, draws, and calls us, and He is called the Counselor, the Comforter, our Teacher who leads and guides us into all truth, and many other attributes. He is the Spirit of joy, the Spirit of peace, the Spirit of grace, and the Spirit of truth. We are not to grieve the Holy Spirit, which also tells us that the Holy Spirit is a person and has feelings just like the Father and the Son have feelings. Holy Spirit is perfect love like God the Father and Jesus, and we do not need to fear Him. We do not have to be cautious with the Holy Spirit, as some pastors falsely warn. God requires a deep respect for the Holy Spirit when He warns about sinning against the Holy Spirit. Blasphemy against the Holy Spirit is unforgivable. The Holy Spirit is *the Promise* or the promised Holy Spirit in the book of Acts and elsewhere in scripture (Acts 1:4; 2:33, 39). He is personal to us.

Before we get into the calling or drawing of the Holy Spirit, there are a few other facts we need to address. Salvation is all about what has been done for us by God through Jesus and the Holy Spirit. It has nothing to do with what we have done. We cannot even pay for a small part of it. It was purchased and paid in full by the redemptive work of Jesus the day He suffered and died on our behalf. It is a gift. And, gifts must be received, which is our part; *it needs to be accepted.*

Jesus was without sin, so He was the only one able to pay for our salvation. We are not without sin and therefore are unable to purchase anything from God who is completely holy. It is all paid for by Jesus. His suffering on the Cross, His death, His resurrection, and His ascension provide all we need. It is nothing of our actions but all of Christ. However, we do have a part. I repeat, we need to *receive* this incredible gift of grace by faith, which involves complete trust in Jesus and His sacrificial work on the

Cross. Jesus paid a high price for our salvation, and we can add nothing to earn even a tiny part. It is a paid-in-full gift from God. *"For it is by grace you have been saved, through faith—and this not of yourselves, it is a gift of God—not by works, so that no one can boast"* (Eph. 2:8, 9; NIV).

Each one of us is born in sin because of the fall of man. The first man and woman disobeyed God, and that is how sin entered the world. As a consequence, each one of us is born with a sinful nature. No one needs to teach us how to do wrong; we naturally sin because it is our inherited nature. We were also created with the ability to make choices. If we could not make decisions, we would not be able to choose loving God. Without the ability to accept Him, there could not be a meaningful relationship. Real relationships exist when two individuals mutually decide to love each other. Christianity is not about religion but relationship.

God's desire is for us to choose Him so that those deep relationships can happen. In the beginning, man chose to disobey God and broke up the relationship. The breaking of a relationship with God is called spiritual death in the Bible. But God has provided a way to restore the relationship with Him. God was gracious and sent His Son to pay the redeeming price, enabling us to be restored in relationship with God. Jesus's death on the Cross is God's gift of grace, and we need to receive this grace through faith, as was just quoted above in Ephesians 2:8.

Our part is to believe, receiving this gift of God by faith, trusting God that He provided, and paid the price for us to be in a relationship with Him. Within the church, there is a lack of understanding that we need to accept or receive Jesus into our lives, making a full surrender. In the church, we frequently hear about Jesus and His death on the Cross, which is where it usually ends. The prevailing thought is, He did it all, and that settles it. Our part in receiving is not emphasized enough in many churches. Some claim that since Jesus did it all, which is correct as far as paying the price is concerned, we don't need to do anything. But we do need to do something; we must repent of our sins and receive this extravagant gift, surrendering our lives to Him. A gift is of no value if it is not accepted, unwrapped, and used. Good teaching will include both what God has done and what man must do. It is not automatic from merely knowing about Jesus. "Yet to all who *received him,* to those who believed in his name, he gave the right to become children of God" (John 1:12; NIV, my emphasis).

We will go on to unwrap many of the benefits of the gift of receiving Christ and explore the richness of what it means to believe. The Bible has much to say about believing in the Lord and being saved. It is far more than accepting the right teachings. Nor is believing just thinking correctly in your head and merely giving mental assent to the fact. The devil also believes and knows all about Jesus dying and paying the price, and he is not saved and will never receive salvation. In James 2:19 (NIV), the Bible says, "You believe that there is one God. Good! Even the demons believe that and shudder."

It is of eternal consequence as to how we believe. Good teaching explains both God's work and the requirements on our part.

Before we become a Christian, the Holy Spirit is at work calling us and drawing us to Christ. "For no one can come to me unless the Father who sent me draws them to me, and on the last day I will raise them up" (John 6:44; NLT). And in John 6:63, 64, the Word tells us, "It is the Spirit who gives eternal life. Human effort accomplishes nothing. And the words I have spoken to you are spirit and life. But some of you do not believe me." Immediately, following that statement, Jesus says, "That is what I meant when I said that people can't come to me unless the Father brings them to me" (John 6:65; NLT).

When the Holy Spirit works in us, tugging at our hearts, we know that He is drawing us to Himself.

> "All of us both Jews and Gentiles must come to the Father through the same Holy Spirit because of what Christ has done for us" (Eph. 2:18; NLT).

> For when we brought you the Good News, it was not only with words but also with power for the Holy Spirit gave you full assurance that what we said was true. (1 Thess. 1:5; NLT).

According to these verses, we cannot be saved without the drawing of the Holy Spirit. The drawing and calling is the pre-salvation work of the Spirit. Obviously, the calling or the drawing of the Spirit is critical. Conviction is the love-pull of God. Praise Him! And, conviction happens when hearing the Word of God. Hearing the Gospel is necessary.

It is the power of the Holy Spirit who convicts us of sin and our need for Christ in our hearts, not just in our heads, which is merely mental assent. The Spirit calls us, inviting us into a relationship with Jesus, to know Him intimately at the heart level.

Often Christianity is reduced to a mere religion or philosophy like all other religions rather than an intimate, loving relationship with Jesus. If we are in love with Jesus, there is no problem in obeying Him; being in love, we desire to please Him in whatever He wants. When we fall in love with another person, we will do anything to enhance our relationship with them. That is the way it is when you fall in love with Jesus; you will do anything to please Him to demonstrate how much you love Him. It's a longing of the heart from a loving relationship rather than following rules and completing obligations.

How are we drawn to Jesus by the Spirit? There are various ways in which the Spirit calls us. Most of the time, we are drawn through hearing the Word of God in multiple ways. Romans 10:17 (NIV) says, "Faith comes from hearing the message, and the message is heard through the word about Christ." That hearing can happen in several ways like the preaching of the Word, listening to music, hearing testimonies, reading Christian materials, radio broadcasts, podcasts, and watching Christian television. When the Holy Spirit draws and calls, make sure you do not harden your heart, resisting the drawing of the Spirit. "So as the Holy Spirit says: Today if you hear his voice, do not harden your hearts" (Heb. 3:7, 8) and repeats itself in verse 15 and again in 4:7. When we hear the Gospel, the Holy Spirit convicts us of our need for Jesus in our life. When the Spirit is calling, you need to open your heart to the calling of God on your life.

Conviction is not something negative but is a love-call, inviting us to come into an intimate relationship with the King of kings and the Lord of lords, which results in abundant life. Unfortunately, the drawing or calling by the Holy Spirit is absent in a large segment of Christian teaching. We make up simple formulas that instruct us to pray a simple prayer without any conviction, commitment, or surrender and then attempt to convince people they are now on the way to heaven. Instead, it is all about Jesus entering the heart and coming into a personal relationship with Him. Knowing God is so much more than mere knowledge about Him; it is to have fellowship with Him. When you receive Christ under the conviction of the Holy Spirit, the result is a life-changing conversion often missed. Holy Spirit conviction is your friend. The working of the Holy Spirit is essential in true conversion. You need to expose yourself to the operation of the Holy Spirit. Are you in such a place or such a church?

Many in our churches have a fear of testimonies and altar calls because it makes them very uncomfortable. It was very uncomfortable for me too. A conviction may seem painful but is the loving call of the Father. He loves you and desires you to become His son or daughter. That discomfort is the Holy Spirit drawing and calling us out of the darkness. Darkness does not like light. Even churchy people become uneasy when hearing testimonies for various reasons. Some people have never experienced the working of the Spirit in their lives and do not realize that something is missing; no one wants to admit that. Many have only assumed they were saved and take offense at hearing a story of genuine conversion. People have a comfortable knowledge about God but do not have a personal relationship with the Lord and are convicted. Others, like myself, understand that I need this for myself but resist because of fearing the loss of worldly pleasure. When a real conviction is taking place, be assured the enemy will also be at work, attempting to destroy the work of the Spirit, telling you not to surrender.

Opportunities need to be provided for the Spirit to knock at the door of one's heart. Do you see people at the altar in your church on any given Sunday, repenting and inviting Jesus into their hearts? There should be an opportunity to respond to the message delivered. The response is part of worship. The Gospel needs a presentation that is captivating, welcoming, and loving. We want to reach those who are not in a relationship with the Lord, but do we know how to do it? Some say let's keep it low key, so we attract seekers and don't turn them off. If the full Gospel is taught and lived, there will be no problem attracting "seekers." Being seeker-friendly should never sacrifice the power of the Gospel, lest we become a club, and we lose everything.

The church has mission statements like "Reaching the Lost for Christ," which is excellent, but we need to reach the lost in our church membership also. I have visited many churches and have never heard a genuine conversion testimony. Why would we go out to reach the lost when people within the church have never received Jesus as Lord? Perhaps we should learn how to reach the lost at home first. Yes, a genuine conversion is necessary for everyone. Jesus said, "You must be born again." From that statement, it is clear there is no such thing as having been born a Christian. Therefore, it is impossible to have been a Christian for all of your life, which many proclaim. Being born again is not a process; it is a birth. It takes place in a moment, just like physical birth. That is why Jesus used the expression, born again. Listen to the calling of the Spirit. He will call, provided you put yourself in a position to hear the Gospel.

The drawing or calling requires a response. The Holy Spirit is continually calling many, but few respond. Because of the lack of sound teaching, many do not know what to do when the Spirit is calling. As I shared in my testimony, I did not know or recognize what the Spirit was up to when I felt so drawn to Him.

Jesus made a remarkable and revealing statement in Matthew 22:14: "For many are called, but few are chosen." Many are being called to the wedding of the lamb, but few accept the invitation for various reasons. But, these excuses will mean nothing on the day of His return and will bring great sorrow. Jesus made many shocking statements concerning who will and will not be saved. We need to read the Bible for ourselves to arrive at the truth.

Questions for discussion:

1. Have you experienced Jesus tugging at your heart? What was it like?
2. Did you experience any resistance in your heart?

3. How do you feel about Matthew 22:14? Which camp are you in?

4. Read Matthew 7:13–14; what is your reaction to the entrance being narrow?

5. What impact does the statement, "only a few will find it" (the entrance) have on you?

6. How have you experienced the calling or the drawing of the Spirit in your life? Explain.

CHAPTER 4

REPENTANCE

"Unless you repent, you too will all perish" (Luke 13:3).

W hen we travel, we often encounter signs which warn of certain dangers. The warning signs are for our protection. As we went to the Grand Canyon on vacation, we saw signs warning about watching your children so they would not fall over the edge, down into the canyon, which would be certain death. The warning in Luke 13:3 is a love-warning, hoping no one will perish. We do not have to obey the warning sign if that is our choice. However, the consequences are grievous.

What is repentance? The dictionary in my Bible states, "To experience sorrow for and seek to change wrong behavior." Webster's dictionary says, "to feel so contrite over one's sins as to change or decide to change one's ways; be penitent." Using simple language, it means to do a one-eighty; to turn and go in the opposite direction. Initially, there must be a firm-enough conviction of sin to enable a person to change one's ways. That is the work of the Holy Spirit (John 16:8). One person can beat another over the head with the Bible but will never be able to create a deep sorrow in someone over their sins. Only the Spirit can perform such a supernatural feat. However, most often, the Holy Spirit uses Scripture to convict a person in a way that leads to repentance. The Holy Spirit will also simultaneously convince an individual of God's lavish love. The conviction of sin and, at the same time, God's loving call is an unusual mix. Often the ingredient of love is left out of conviction. The powerful realization of God's love is enough to overcome the work of the enemy, regardless of the grip evil may have on a life.

Initially, the thought of repentance is not very affirming or positive, but true repentance involves the powerful force of love. It is an invitation from the living God, the Lord of all, to come to Him. There is no invitation equal to the offer of the gift of eternal life. This life is not only an offer for the unseen future but an offer of abundant life right now. You are most blessed to receive such conviction and convincing of God's desire for anyone. Have you received such love? If not, are you willing to accept such love? We need to be confident that God, through the Holy Spirit, loves us more than we can comprehend and that God has the best plan for our life.

Because of the firm grip of darkness, turning around and going in the opposite direction appears to be painful and undesirable, but it is God's love for us that enables us to make the hurdle.

> God's kindness is intended to lead you to repentance. (Rom. 2:4; NIV)

> Godly sorrow brings repentance that leads to salvation and leaves no regret, but worldly sorrow brings death. See what this godly sorrow had produced in you: what earnestness, what eagerness to clear yourselves, what indignation, what alarm,

what longing, what concern, what readiness to see justice done. (2 Cor. 7:10; NIV)

The verse brings up godly sorrow and earthly sorrow. Godly sorrow is the work of the Holy Spirit. Godly sorrow often produces tears of sorrow over sin. Such sorrow over my sins and the recognition of God's love for me was so overwhelming that tears flowed as I surrendered my life to Him. Repentance and receiving Christ as Lord of my life was the most significant moment in my life, paving the way for many more beautiful moments.

At Pentecost, when Peter preached and explained what was happening, people were cut to the heart and asked: "Brothers, what must we do?" "Peter replied, 'Repent, and let every one of you be baptized in the name of Jesus Christ for the remission of sins'" (Acts 2:38; NKJV).

Without repentance, we continue in our sin of serving self. We need to turn around, away from our sin of self-centeredness, and make the decision to follow Jesus. That is the one-eighty we need to take. When coming to Christ, it is good to take time to invite the Holy Spirit to bring to mind all known sins, confessing them, and then asking for forgiveness of each wrongdoing. The reward will be a cherished freedom.

While Peter was addressing the return of Jesus, he makes the following statement regarding repentance. "The Lord isn't really being slow about his promise, as some people think. No, he is being patient for your sake. He does not want anyone to be destroyed, but wants everyone to repent" (2 Pet. 3:9; NLT).

God's will and desire are for everyone to come to Him in repentance before He returns.

Repentance also needs to be practiced as we journey through life until the day of His return. In Psalm 51, David, a man after God's own heart, cries out to God for forgiveness after sinning. He pleads for God's mercy and forgiveness. He goes to great length to confess his sin and the evil in his heart. David goes on, requesting God not to take away the Holy Spirit from him and to restore the joy of his salvation. He asks for the ability to continue praising God. This example is one of the best examples in Scripture of real repentance.

In Revelation 2:4–5, 7 (NLT), there is another example of God requiring repentance on the part of those who are believers:

> But I have this complaint against you. You don't love me or each other as you did at first! Look how far you have fallen! Turn back to me and do the works you did at first. If you don't repent, I will come and remove your lampstand from its place among the churches. … To all who are victorious, I will give fruit from the tree of life in the paradise of God.

Repentance is necessary whenever we are convicted of sin in our lives. If we are in love with God, it is no longer challenging to confess sins; in fact, we desire to maintain a deep relationship. Repentance brings freedom from the bondage we experience from our sinfulness. "If we confess our sins, he is faithful and just and will forgive us our sins and purify us from all unrighteousness" (1 John 1:9; NIV).

God is so gracious in forgiving us our sins when we ask with a repentant heart. His love and grace is a gift of such magnitude that we really cannot comprehend it with the human mind. Praise Him for forgiveness when we repent. Repentance is a loving invitation to restore fellowship with a loving Father. When we sin, we have an advocate with the Father in our defense—Jesus Christ (1 John 2:1). A lifestyle of quick repentance, when convicted of sin, leads to a life of continual fellowship and confidence in the Father in answering our prayers. (There is more on a deeper level of repentance in the chapter on preparing to receive the baptism in the Holy Spirit.)

Questions for discussion:

1. Have you ever considered God's requirement of repentance an act of love?
2. Do you consider Holy Spirit's conviction of sin a love-call?
3. Why do we resist repentance when God calls it His kindness? (See Rom. 2:4)
4. How does 1 John 1:9 encourage you to repent?

CHAPTER 5

BORN OF THE SPIRIT

∽૦∾

"Jesus said, 'Unless one is born again he cannot see the kingdom of God'" (John 3:3; NLT).

When we sense the drawing or calling of the Spirit, we need to respond. If you have experienced the Holy Spirit pulling on your heartstrings, He is attempting to convince you to receive Christ. That tugging on your heart is the most incredible invitation you will ever get. God is drawing you to Himself because He loves you lavishly and is inviting us into a relationship with Him. Without Jesus in our hearts, we are spiritually dead and in desperate need of His indwelling. Jesus wants us to be spiritually alive in Him; that is why He calls us. We need forgiveness and a change of heart to proceed in the opposite direction. The Spirit is the helper in receiving Christ Jesus.

The initial biblical response to His invitation is to repent, to believe, and to receive.

To repent means to turn around and go in the opposite direction. We need to understand that we are all born with a sinful nature, and in the flesh, we naturally sin. Romans 3:23, 24 (NIV) says, "For all have sinned and fall short of the glory of God, and are justified freely by His grace through the redemption that came by Christ Jesus."

We are born with a sin problem and need redemption. Romans 6:23 NIV says, "For the wages of sin is death (spiritual separation from God), but the gift of God is eternal life in Christ Jesus, our Lord." Man is naturally sinful and separated from God. Therefore, man cannot know and experience the love of God and His beautiful plan for each life without Jesus.

To believe is to place all of your trust in Jesus and His work for us on the Cross. It is not mental assent. It is nothing of ourselves nor any good works. To believe is to be steadfast in adhering to the gospel, trusting in everything that Jesus taught, and complete reliance on His faithfulness while you obediently follow Him in all He has commanded. Studying scripture reveals much about the richness of the word *believe*.

To receive Jesus is to sincerely invite Him into your life by surrendering your life to Him as the Holy Spirit draws you to Him. Receiving Him into your heart allows the Holy Spirit to take up residence in your heart, giving you full assurance that you are His forever.

The chasm between a holy God and a sinful man is more massive than we can comprehend. Man is continually trying to reach out to God through his efforts. The attempts are impossible, and the only way to reach out to God is to receive the gift of eternal life for which Jesus paid the ultimate price on the Cross. God loves us so much that He gave His one and only Son as a sacrifice to pay for our sin. The Bible explains that only Jesus, who was without sin, could pay the price of our sin. John 3:16 says that "God so loved the world that He gave His one and only Son, that whoever believes in Him shall not perish but have eternal life."

He not only paid the price for our sin, but He also died and rose from the grave so we can have an abundant life right now.

"Jesus said, 'I came that they might have life, and might have it abundantly'" (John 10:10; NIV).

Because of our sinfulness and God's holiness, the Father has provided a way of forgiveness and eternal life for anyone willing to receive. Jesus, who being perfect, is the only one who is able and did pay for our sins and is the only provision the Father has provided. Jesus said, "I am the way, and the truth, and the life: no one comes to the Father but through me" (John 14:6).

Only Jesus can bridge the vast chasm separating us from God. The reason that Jesus is the only way is that in our sinful nature, we can never accomplish the righteousness of God. God is holy with no darkness in Him at all, and we are fallen, sinful creatures. But, God, in absolute fairness, sent His Son who was perfect, to pay the penalty for our sin and place each person who receives Jesus into their life, in right standing with the Father.

We must individually receive Jesus Christ as Savior, Lord, and King of our lives. "As many as received Him, to them He gave the right to become children of God, even to those who believe in His name" (John 1:12). We receive through faith, trusting that He will do what He said. "For it is by grace you have been saved through faith; and that not of yourselves, it is the gift of God; not as a result of works, so that no one may boast" (Eph. 2:8, 9; NASB).

When we invite Christ into our lives in faith, completely trusting Him to do it, He comes to live in our hearts through the Holy Spirit. It is His Spirit, the Holy Spirit, who takes up residence in our hearts. We will then know and experience the love of the Father and begin to grow in the grace and knowledge of Jesus.

If you do not have a personal relationship with Jesus, actually knowing Him, you can invite Him into your heart by praying a prayer something like this:

> Lord Jesus, I need you! I am a sinner, and I thank
> you for paying the price on the Cross for my sins.
> I ask you to forgive me of all my sins and come to
> live in my heart. I open the door of my heart and
> let you come in so that I may know you intimately.
> I fully surrender my life to you! You may have con-
> trol of my life from this day forward. Have your
> way in me, Jesus! Take control of my life! Holy
> Spirit, Spirit of Jesus, come and live in me taking
> control of my life! Thank you, Jesus, for forgiving
> me of my sins and giving me eternal life! Create
> in me a new heart, oh God, and make me a new
> person in Christ Jesus. Thank you, Jesus!

Sincerely praying that kind of prayer *and* opening your heart to Jesus permits Jesus to come and live in your heart. He loves you deeply. If you prayed that prayer sincerely, you are now His son or daughter, an adopted child of God!

> Look! I stand at the door and knock. If you hear
> my voice and open the door, I will come in, and we
> will share a meal together as friends. Those who
> are victorious will sit with me on my throne just
> as I was victorious and sat with my Father on his
> throne. (Rev. 3:20, 21; NLT)

In your Bible, write down the date you received Christ into your heart and tell others what you did because it is with the mouth that you profess your faith and are saved (Rom. 10:10). You will be affirmed and blessed! Congratulations, you're a child of the living God and have an impressive inheritance! Becoming a child of God is not anywhere near the end. Becoming His child is just the start of abundant life. Ahead of you, there is more excitement in following Jesus than we can imagine!

We will take a close look at more scripture to see some of the things that happen when we are born of the Holy Spirit. First, when reading the gospel of John, you only have to get to chapter 3, and you will see other expressions that are equivalent to that expression, such as "born of the Holy Spirit." "Born again" is perhaps the most frequently used. Born from above and born of God are other expressions, all meaning the same thing. Each one adds insight into the full meaning of the speech. "Born of the Spirit" gives insight into the sense that it is a work of the Spirit. The phrase *born again* provides the insight that it must happen after physical birth and is birth but not the same as physical birth. Born of God means it is His work in us and not of self-effort. "Flesh gives birth to flesh, but the Spirit gives birth to spirit" (John 3:6 NIV). God's Word is very rich in meaning.

There are many scriptures which enlighten us as to what happens when we are born again. You enter the kingdom of God, according to John 3:3. You become a new creature in Christ Jesus. All things become new, and the old passes away (1 Cor. 5:17). We have access to the Father (Eph. 2:18). You are predestined to become like Jesus (Rom. 8:29). You are being sanctified (set apart) by the Holy Spirit (2 Thess. 2:13; 1 Thess. 5:23). You will hear and know His voice (John 10:16, 27). You will gain knowledge of God the Father and Jesus (John 10:14, 15). You are having a place prepared for you in heaven (John 14:1). Jesus will come back to receive you and take you with Him to heaven at the end of this age (John 14:2). He gives you a deep hunger and appreciation for scripture (Psalm 1:2). You will love Him with heartfelt worship (Rev. 5:11–14; 22:17). You will have an eagerness for His return (Heb. 9:28; 2 Tim. 4:8). You will have concern for the lost and hurting (Matt. 25:31–46). The Holy Spirit becomes your Teacher, leading and guiding you into all truth. There are many more in scripture. Read John, chapters 14–17, and you will say, "Whoa, man, far out!"

When challenging most people about being born again, the typical response is, "Well, I didn't have a Damascus Road conversion or anything like it, but I think I'm saved, at least I sure hope so." That is an open door to share what Jesus has done in your life. But, the question concerning the Damascus Road conversion needs an explanation. First, the bright light shining on Paul and the voice he heard was not the conversion. That reality is how God got his attention. The transformation is what happened in the heart; the 180-degree turn in his life from persecuting Christians to becoming one of them and becoming the persecuted one himself, spending much time in various prisons. The conversion is always what takes place in the heart, from what it was to what it has become. The drastic change in Paul's life on the Damascus Road is not the light and the voice, nor even the healing that followed. Each one of us must have such a turn-around in life. Conversion is the change in our belief system, resulting in action on that belief. We all need a Damascus Road conversion.

My observation and experience are that genuine rebirth occurs when we receive Christ while under Holy Spirit conviction, making a full surrender to the Lordship of Jesus. It does not matter if you are churched or unchurched; such conversion produces a person on fire for Jesus and crazy in love with Him. In our culture, we like to find the minimum requirement to stay out of hell. Fire insurance against the fires of hell is what many desire. Permit me to be bold; there is no such thing! Jesus is either Lord of all or not Lord at all, as the saying goes. If you are looking for a minimum requirement merely to get by, you need to have a serious study of God's Word and an honest heart talk with God. It is a contradiction to be in a loving relationship with Jesus and simultaneously desire a minimal relationship, merely getting to heaven.

When I was dating my wife before marriage and falling in love with her, I naturally wanted to please her, even doing little extra things that would bring her joy and make her smile. I would go so far as to ask other gals what she would like for a gift at Christmas time and other appropriate times because I wanted to know what would please her the most and what would make her the happiest. It was a joy to please her and certainly not looked at as something I had to do. It was because of love that I wanted to bless her. I certainly wasn't looking to the minimum so I could "get by." Why would it be any different in loving Jesus?

Unfortunately, many no longer teach, "You must be born again." In fact, in infant baptism, it is often said, "now, the baby is sealed by the Holy Spirit and is marked by God." At a person's funeral, it is said that the person was sealed by the Holy Spirit when they were baptized as a baby. Read your Bible! This is false teaching! If that is the case, according to scripture, the baby is saved when baptized as an infant because the Spirit indwells the child (Rom. 8:9). With such instruction, there is no need to teach being born again since it happened in infant baptism. But, Jesus said, "You must be born again (John 3:3). That can only occur when a person personally receives Christ. The Bible says that the Holy Spirit enters a person when they receive the gift of eternal life.

> And you also were included in Christ when you heard the message of truth, the gospel of your salvation. *When you believed,* you were marked in him with a seal, the promised Holy Spirit, who is a deposit guaranteeing our inheritance until the redemption of those who are God's possession—to

the praise of his glory. (Eph. 1:13–14; NIV, my emphasis)

It is clear that when you come to Christ, you are marked and sealed by the Holy Spirit, not when you have been baptized as an infant. Each person must personally receive Christ into their heart. An infant is not capable of receiving Christ.

When the Holy Spirit enters your heart, it becomes natural to love and follow Jesus. Your nature will be changed entirely with desires opposite of what it had been before you received Christ. The sad thing is many do not know when the new birth took place because of the lack of teaching and understanding of being born again. Consequently, there is also a severe lack of assurance of salvation. Some assume salvation happened someplace along life's path, which is even worse. The subject of being born of the Holy Spirit needs a detailed study because of the eternal consequences.

The lack of knowledge in the church is alarming, to put it mildly. If you are not sure of salvation, please go back to the prayer on receiving Jesus and make sure. It is better to pray it an extra time than to miss out on a relationship with Jesus. If you have that relationship and are confident, it is not required to pray such a prayer again, but to continue believing God and His Word. He will come into your heart if you are serious. The feeling of assurance will eventually happen if not immediately. Emotions are not your guarantee, even though love is a feeling and will occur as the relationship grows.

There is an alternative to receiving Christ into your heart, your spirit, or your innermost being. The only other option is not to accept Him. We need to count the cost of accepting Jesus, which may be ridicule or some form of persecution. But we need to calculate the price of not receiving Him also, which is eternal separation from God. And, to do nothing is the same as not receiving;

the consequences of both are severe—the cost of not accepting Jesus far outweighs the cost of receiving Christ.

Why do people not receive Jesus or put it off, not taking it seriously? The Bible says that people love darkness more than light. They are in darkness and do not understand the light nor the blessings of being in the light. People do not know the joy of the Spirit because if you do not have the Spirit, you do not understand the things of the Spirit. Those who refuse feel they are having real joy because sin is fun for a season and do not want to leave it. There may be addictions of various kinds that are too difficult to break by their power, and they give up. Many are afraid of what others will think of them if they become a Christian. Satan simply puts fear into their hearts.

Some people feel they are pretty good and that it is not necessary to complete all this Christian stuff. They only hope they will make it to heaven someday, without absolute assurance of salvation. There exists the feeling that everything will be okay even if they do not receive Him. The real reason is unbelief, and only the Spirit can convict and convince people of the need for Jesus in their hearts. There is a complete void in understanding that Jesus will return, and we all will face judgment. There is none or little instruction on the end times preceding the second coming, which results in no conviction to get right with God.

When a person receives Christ, there is great rejoicing in heaven (Luke 15:4–7). If you have just accepted Christ, there is a party going on in heaven. At the same time, the powers of darkness are not so excited about your decision as those in heaven. In reality, you have a new enemy (Eph. 6:12; 1 Pet. 5:8). When you are of the world, Satan does not need to deal with you, except to encourage you to be at enmity with the kingdom of God. He pretty much uses the same bag of tricks, actually lies. He will tell you, "Your decision was not real. You are not a child of God." Satan will make up all kinds of lies to try to convince you that you are a fake and that it is not real.

Satan is the great deceiver and the father of lies (Rev. 13:14; 20:3). Tell him, out loud, to leave and that God's Word says that you are His child and that He is faithful to His Word. Declare His Word and promises over yourself. Your testimony and the blood of Jesus will defeat him (Rev. 12:11). Persecution will come your way (2 Tim. 3:12). The powers of darkness will activate anyone against you; they possibly can. But, "Greater is He that is within you (the Holy Spirit) than he that is in the world (the powers of darkness)" (1 John 4:4).

Romans 8:38–39 reads, "For I am convinced that neither death nor life, neither angels nor demons, neither the present nor the future, nor any powers, neither height nor depth, nor anything else in all creation, will be able to separate us from the love of God that is in Christ Jesus our Lord." When you are persecuted, remember, your reward is great.

The secret to being born again is inviting and allowing Jesus to take up residence in your heart through the Holy Spirit. "For God wanted them to know that the riches and glory of Christ are for you Gentiles, too. *And this is the secret: Christ lives in you.* This assures you of sharing his glory" (Col. 1:27; NLT, my emphasis). The Holy Spirit must indwell you, or you have not been saved. "You, however, are not in the realm of the flesh but are in the realm of the Spirit, if indeed the Spirit of God lives in you. And if anyone does not have the Spirit of Christ, they do not belong to Christ" (Rom. 8:9; NIV).

It is necessary to know the Lord, not merely to know about Him. Jesus said, "And this is the way to have eternal life—to know you, the only true God, and Jesus Christ, the one you sent to earth" (John 17:3; NLT).

Questions for discussion:

1. In John 3:3, why does Jesus use the expression, "born again?"
2. To you personally, what does it mean to be born again? (John 3:3–8).
3. Is it possible to be born a Christian or to be a Christian all of your life?
4. Name some reasons why people do not understand the new birth.
5. What takes place in a life when a person is born again?
6. List some things that happen to you when you are born again?
7. Name some equivalent expression to being born again?

CHAPTER 6

ASSURANCE OF SALVATION

ແ໐໐

"I write these things to you who believe in the name of the son of God so that you may know that you have eternal life" (1 John 5:13; NIV).

There are so many who have no biblical assurance of salvation. Also, many in the church have a false assurance of salvation, which is more challenging to deal with than no confidence. Many in the church feel that they are going to heaven because of their belief system, which may be their denominational doctrines, their church teachings, or their perceived understanding. Often, we think that whatever we have been taught or born into is the correct belief system. We call these systems systematic theology which has us look at and interpret scripture through a given lens. Everyone tends to believe the way they were taught, thinking that their method of theology is the correct one. As mentioned earlier, we have thousands of denominations, each one offering something different from every other denomination. How can this be the truth? At best, only one out of thousands could be correct on all issues, and that probability is extremely low, near zero. These differences should awaken us to a serious study of scripture.

There are many false assurances of salvation that seem good and reasonable to humankind. Many believe that since they were born into a Christian family or even a Christian nation like the United States, or they grew up as a Christian, makes one a Christian. Other reasons are as follows: having a Christian education; being a deacon, elder, Sunday school teacher, or a pastor; having attended church, receiving good teaching all of their life; having memorized a lot of scripture; living a good moral life and performing many good deeds. The truth is that if any of these deeds could save us, Jesus would not have had to endure the tremendous suffering of dying on the Cross.

Unfortunately, a lot of people, in some way, have been convinced or talked into believing they are a Christian. A high percentage of people also believe that if they never committed a grave sin like committing adultery, robbing a bank, or killing someone that they will go to heaven. There seems to be no understanding that we are born in sin and are unable to pay for our sins. Only Jesus can pay for our sins, which requires a perfect sacrifice to a holy God, and only Jesus is perfect, without sin.

> For there is no difference; for all have sinned and
> fall short of the glory of God. (Rom. 3:23; NIV)

> For the wages of sin is death, but the gift of God
> is eternal life in Christ Jesus our Lord. (Rom.
> 6:23; NIV)

Even knowing all the facts about ourselves and salvation that we are born in sin, our need to repent, having full knowledge of the sacrifice of Jesus's death on the cross, and believing all about Jesus is not the biblical assurance of salvation. You may have always attended church and know all the answers. This belief is probably one of the most common false assurances of salvation. Remember that even Satan and all his demons believe that. They believe it so firmly that they tremble and shudder.

> Jesus said to the Pharisees, the most religious and most learned of all people, "You do not have his message in your hearts, because you do not believe me—the one he sent to you. You search the Scriptures because you think they give you eternal life. But the Scriptures point to me! Yet you refuse to come to me to receive this life." (John 5:38, 39; NLT)

The false assurance from the lack of knowledge of scripture, without Jesus living in you, is often called "the spirit of religion" and is very deceptive because it appears legitimate. The evil "spirit of religion" reduces the relationship with Jesus to a religion of rules like all other religions in the world. We need the living Jesus in our hearts, resulting in a new life. We must be aware of the many false assurances of salvation, even in our churches. The Bible has much instruction concerning false teaching.

What does Jesus mean in John 5:38, 39, when He said, "You do not have His message in your hearts, because you do believe me"? He is saying that He never got into their hearts; it was only in their minds from all the study they did. That does not mean you should not study but that the Bible explains that Jesus needs to get into your heart. There is a tremendous difference between head knowledge and heart knowledge.

"To them, God willed to make known what are the riches of the glory of this mystery among the Gentiles: which is *Christ in you*, the hope of glory" (Col. 1:27; NKJV, my emphasis). It is Christ in you that is necessary, which means the Spirit of Jesus is in you, which is the Holy Spirit. The Holy Spirit must have taken up residence in your heart. The New Testament says over and over that the indwelling of the Holy Spirit is our assurance of salvation. What that means is that the Spirit of Christ, the Spirit of God, which is the Holy Spirit, needs to get into your spirit or heart.

The Bible goes so far as to instruct us that if the Holy Spirit is not in us, then we are not a Christian at all. "But you are not controlled by your sinful nature. You are controlled by the Spirit if you have the Spirit of God living in you. *And remember that those who do not have the Spirit of Christ living in them do not belong to him at all"* (Rom. 8:9; NLT, my emphasis).

The biblical assurance of salvation is the Holy Spirit in you. The Holy Spirit is the earnest or the down payment, guaranteeing that we belong to Him.

> He anointed us, set his seal of ownership on us, and put His Spirit in our hearts as a deposit, guaranteeing what is to come. (2 Cor. 1:22; NIV)

> Now it is God who has made us for this very purpose and has given us the Spirit as a deposit, guaranteeing what is to come. (2 Cor. 5:5; NIV)

Ephesians 1:13, 14 (NIV) explains clearly how we come to Christ by hearing the truth of the gospel and that we are sealed by the Holy Spirit when we believe: "And you also were included in Christ when you heard the word of truth, the gospel of your salvation. Having believed you were marked in Him with a seal, the promised Holy Spirit, who is a deposit guaranteeing our inheritance until the redemption of those who are God's possession to the praise of His glory." Read carefully and notice when you respond to the gospel by believing, that is when the Holy Spirit seals you, not when you are born or baptized as an infant, as some teach. Such teaching is not the Word of God, but the philosophy of man.

While serving on the staff in our church, I visited a lady who was over ninety years old and of sound mind. She was very well educated and knowledgeable of scripture. In fact, in her life, she had memorized half of the Psalms. As I was visiting her in the hospital while she was on her death bed, she told me that "dying is hard work." In her struggle, I tried to assure her of the presence of the Lord. As we talked, she said that she did not experience the presence of the Holy Spirit. As I continued to ask questions, she admitted that she never asked Jesus into her heart. After further explanation, I led her in a prayer to invite Jesus into her heart. After she prayed, she suddenly began to praise the Lord by saying over and over with genuine excitement, "Thank you, Jesus, thank you, Jesus, thank you, Jesus!" The joy and excitement she exhibited were very enthusiastic. She continued praising Jesus for two days and then entered eternity saved and sealed by the Holy Spirit. Her joy was so exuberant that people asked what happened to her. She was born of the Holy Spirit!

What the Bible Tells Us Concerning the Assurance of Salvation

Watch for the common denominator in all of these verses. It is always the presence of the Holy Spirit.

> "He has identified us as His own by placing the Holy Spirit in our hearts as the first installment that guarantees everything He has promised us" (2 Cor. 1:22; NLT).

The Bible says the indwelling Holy Spirit is our guarantee of all he has promised. Again it says,

> "God Himself has prepared us for this, and as a guarantee He has given us His Holy Spirit" (2 Cor. 5:5; NLT).

The Holy Spirit is also called the Spirit of God and the Spirit of God's Son, Jesus.

> "And because we are His children, God has sent the Spirit of His Son into our hearts, prompting us to call out, 'Abba Father'" (Gal. 4:6; NLT).

> "And now you Gentiles have also heard the truth, the Good News that God saves you. And when you believed in Christ, He identified you as His own by giving you the Holy Spirit, whom He promised long ago. The Spirit is God's guarantee that He will give us the inheritance He promised and that He has purchased us to be His own people. He did this so we would praise and glorify Him" (Eph. 1:13–14; NLT).

There is so much in those two verses. Notice the Bible repeats; we can be sure of our identity in Him from the indwelling Holy Spirit and that He is our guarantee. It happens when we believe in Him.

> "And we know He lives in us because the Spirit he gave us lives in us" (1 John 3:24b; NLT).

"And God has given us His Spirit as proof that we
live in Him and He in us" (1 John 4:13; NLT).

It should be clear that the Holy Spirit living in us is proof of
our salvation. The Bible offers no other assurance of salvation. It
happens when we put our faith and trust in Jesus as Savior and
Lord. He enters our hearts at the time we surrender under conviction by the Holy Spirit.

We can possess vast knowledge about God, which is not our
assurance of salvation; instead, we need to know Him intimately.
Are you in love with Jesus, the bridegroom? We can study the
scriptures having much knowledge about the Lord, thinking that
is the key, but the scriptures point to Jesus (John 5:38, 39). We
must know the Lord. We need to do more than merely ask Him
into our hearts; we need to open wide the door of our hearts and
allow Him entrance when we invite Him into our hearts. "Behold,
I stand at the door and knock. If anyone hears My voice and opens
the door, I will come into him and dine with him, and he with Me"
(Rev. 3:20; NKJV).

What the Bible explains must happen for the Holy Spirit to enter your heart

Going back to chapter three, you must experience the call of
God on your life. This happens when the Holy Spirit convicts
you of your need for Christ in your life. The verses in John 6
explain that we are unable to come to Jesus unless the Father
draws a person to Him. So this is the first thing that must happen.
One needs to understand they are born in sin and need Christ in
their life.

With that realization, we need to respond by repenting of our
sins and invite Christ into our life, giving Him full control. A

person needs to die to the old life and receive Jesus into their heart in faith, believing. At that point, the Holy Spirit, the Spirit of Jesus, enters your heart, and one is born of the Spirit. When all this is accomplished, a person has full, Biblical assurance of salvation. Then in a surrendered life, a person proceeds in following Jesus in baptism and receiving the Holy Spirit in obedient love.

That is the blessed assurance available to whosoever will come. When Jesus has found entrance into our hearts, we can sing: "Blessed Assurance, Jesus is mine! O what a foretaste of glory divine! Heir of salvation, purchase of God, born of His Spirit, washed in His blood. This is my story; this is my song, Praising my Savior all the day long; this is my story; this is my song, praising my Saviour all the day long" (Fanny Crosby).

Questions for discussion:

1. Before reading this book, what assured you of salvation?
2. What do people, who you know, think assurance of salvation is?
3. List as many false assurances of salvation as you can think of.
4. Is having prayed a prayer for salvation a guarantee you are saved? Explain.
5. What is the biblical assurance of salvation? (Eph. 1:13, 14; 2 Cor. 1:22).
6. "Jesus in you" is the equivalent of the Spirit of Jesus indwelling you (Col. 1:27), do you have the guarantee?

CHAPTER 7

FORGIVENESS
~∽o∽~

**"Forgive us our debts, as we forgive our debtors"
(Matt. 6:12).**

As I mentioned in my testimony, I grew up in a home that was very strict, religious, controlling, and with a father that was abusive, physically and verbally. I wholeheartedly believe my dad was not aware of being offensive, nor did he intend to be rude. In that day, some physical discipline was thought to be the way of disciplining children. The proverb, "Spare the rod and loss the child," was quoted frequently. It was most likely how he was also brought up, so how would he know any different? I also had no idea I was being abused until many years later. At that time, the word *abuse* didn't exist in any vocabularies. I am sure many others have gone through similar treatment in varying degrees while growing up and may have some of the same problems I had.

Abusiveness always leads to a wide assortment of problems and not just a few. Much of my behavior resulted from abuse. I didn't recognize my actions, like anger, as being unusual. When you are young, you don't even know some things you do are a sin. And, some issues do not surface until you grow up, like addictions and other strongholds. Many matters are never recognized, resulting in behaviors with causes unknown to you or others. Sometimes we do not understand why we act or react in specific ways. Often we become the same kind of person as those who brought us up. I decided to never put my children through what I had experienced. But despite my determination, I often found myself acting in much the same way in which I had been treated. It was the way with which I was familiar, and it came naturally.

To break the chain of abuse, someone needs to stop it. I tried hard, but my efforts seemed to accomplish little. I did not initially realize it was a severe evil stronghold and required supernatural power to break it. However, with the help of the Holy Spirit, I was able to break off much of it. My children, I can proudly say, finished breaking the chain. At some point, someone needs to break all chains of evil regardless of the type of bondage. If not, it will continue for generations. If not broken, it will break families down with all kinds of undesirable consequences.

We inherit all kinds of behaviors in addition to being born in sin. We might be curious as to where all these tendencies originate, but more importantly, we need to recognize these sin issues in our lives and what to do about them. The Bible calls these actions deeds of the flesh or following the desires of the sin nature with which we were born.

> When you follow the desires of your sinful nature, the results are very clear: sexual immorality, impurity, lustful pleasures, idolatry, sorcery, hostility, quarreling, jealousy, outbursts of anger, selfish ambition, dissension, division, envy, drunkenness, wild parties, and other sins like these. Let me tell you again, as I have before, that anyone living that

sort of life will not inherit the Kingdom of God.
(Gal. 5:19–21; NLT)

We may have been born with these tendencies, but abuse will significantly enhance these behaviors. For example, if one has lived in an atmosphere of anger, you will more than likely exhibit anger in your life. Bondages, addictions, and strongholds are frequently born out of abuse.

So, if we have this mess in our lives, how do we overcome these tendencies? There is only one answer: the presence of the living Christ in us. Some of my issues were so deep that without the mighty baptism in the Holy Spirit, I would not have been able to overcome. Without the gifts of knowledge and wisdom, it would have been impossible. Hearing the voice of the shepherd, as described in John 10, is a necessity to recognize and receive instruction in defeating sin. It is often not known that without the power of the Holy Spirit, it is impossible to be an overcomer. That is part of the reason Jesus sent the Holy Spirit to give the ability to be victorious in our own lives as well as in helping others.

The Lord knew ahead of time what we would need; therefore, His provisions for us are explicit in scripture. First, one needs the desire to have victory, and that is the most natural part, provided you are in love with Jesus and want to please Him. Ask for wisdom, and He will gladly give it to you (James 1:5). Our need is to forgive those who have wronged us and those we have sinned against, causing divisiveness. Then, we also need to forgive ourselves, which is often the more significant challenge. The Holy Spirit will gladly instruct us to whom we need to make amends. He led me to each one I needed to ask forgiveness. Some were scary to go to and to admit wrongdoings, but the Holy Spirit went ahead of me, preparing hearts. Some were surprised and caught off guard, and others smiled with gratefulness. Every time, healing took place, occasionally with tears, as I offered restitution.

Forgiveness and reconciliation are necessary. The Lord's Prayer says, "Forgive us our trespasses as we forgive those who trespass against us. The Bible says, "If you forgive those who sin against you, your heavenly Father will forgive you. But if you refuse to forgive others, your Father will not forgive your sins" (Matt. 6:14–15; NLT).

I apologized to whomever the Holy Spirit brought to mind whenever it was possible. But I knew I needed to forgive others as well as ask others to forgive me. The greatest struggle was, without a doubt, forgiving my dad. I read all the verses in the Bible about forgiving others. The Bible is clear that we need to forgive if we expect to be forgiven. Our debt to God is infinitely higher than any debt anyone could owe us. Jesus used parables to explain the principle of forgiveness clearly. With Jesus in my life, realizing what He did for me, made forgiveness much more comfortable.

The hurt from my dad was even more profound than I realized. I told God that I forgive him for everything he did and also the devastating words said to me. I also had to overlook the things that he omitted to do. What he did not do was to tell me that he loved me, not even once, nor did he ever put his arms around me as an expression of affection. Because of the deep hurt, I craved affection, to have a glimpse of his caring for me. Everything put together made it hard to forgive as God desires. But, I knew that scripturally I had to forgive him, so I intentionally chose to forgive him for everything. I felt right about that, and it gave me the freedom to not hold anything against him anymore. I realized early on after receiving Christ that I was only making myself miserable by carrying all this junk with me.

I share this not to dishonor my dad. It is not dishonoring to disapprove of someone's wrongdoing. Do not go along with sin in anyone's life, which results in codependency with sin. We do not have to feel self-condemned by the verse that says to honor your father and your mother (Matt. 19:19). It is dishonoring to harbor grudges and return evil by getting back. I believe it is necessary to forgive entirely and to respect parents. We need to honor our parents to the degree that they honor God. We do not need to honor anyone in their evil actions. We need to separate people from their sin, hating their evil while loving the person, including our parents. I know that is not easy, but with the Spirit's help, it can be accomplished. Never call evil good in the name of love.

I recall one Christmas at my parent's house in Montevideo, Minnesota, where my siblings, along with their spouses, and I were sitting around the large dining table visiting, while my parents were sitting around the corner in the living area. The conversation turned spiritual with a concern about healing for a loved one. I shared my testimony concerning salvation and the baptism in the Holy Spirit. I offered assurance from scripture that it was not only all right to pray for healing, but that God desires for us to come to Him for healing. The conversation stimulated a lot of interest and continued for some time. When we finished talking about the baptism in the Holy Spirit and the gifts of the Holy Spirit, I walked into the living room where my dad was sitting, and he obviously listened to the entire conversation we were having. Dad said, "I never want to hear anything like that again." I did not bother to respond, so nothing more was said. My feelings were not hurt, but I felt sorry for him in his strong quenching of the Spirit.

He had always seemed to be a spiritual man and very serious about his faith. I tried several times to enter into a spiritual conversation with him. One time at a very spiritual moment, I asked him if he had ever been born again. He answered without hesitation, giving the place, how it happened, and when. I was so relieved to hear that, despite his bondage to fits of anger. He never experienced deliverance, perhaps due to inadequate teaching. He did know a lot of good stuff but had some spiritual hang-ups.

Dad died suddenly and unexpectedly from a massive heart attack while living in Loveland, Colorado. He was rushed to the hospital and was revived momentarily, but doctors were unable to save him. That was the way he always desired to go, and he got his wish. One of my sisters living in Colorado called me early in the morning to notify me that Dad had died. I had been sleeping and was stunned by the news, and did not respond much. But, many thoughts went through my mind rapidly. It didn't seem possible or real at that moment. I flew to Colorado to help my siblings make arrangements.

My siblings shared with me about Dad reading 1 John 5 for table devotions the night before he died. They shared that he read it in such a way that he knew his time on earth was short. He had given particular emphasis to verse 13, which says, "I write these things to you who believe in the name of the Son of God, so that you may know that you have eternal life." My siblings said it was like he had the assurance that he had eternal life and desired them to have the same confidence. I was able to picture the scene clearly in my mind, the way he always read the Bible at the table.

I had difficulty understanding how anyone could have a genuine encounter with Jesus and still have such bondage to anger when I experienced complete deliverance at the time I received Christ into my heart. With all those conflicting thoughts going through my mind and attempting to process how these two spirits could be coexisting, I shed no tears. I only had grave concern for his salvation. I didn't even shed tears at the funeral except when the pastor shared about Dad's work with the Gideons when the Holy Spirit touched me. I knew of his passion for souls, as I also possessed. He was passionate about speaking in prisons and handing out Bibles, which was encouraging. But I was at peace about my forgiveness of Dad. I had done everything I could think of doing.

It was precisely ten years after my dad died that the Holy Spirit began speaking to me about my relationship with my dad. I thought I had done everything possible, but the Holy Spirit had more for me. My dad died on a Good Friday, and this was the tenth Good Friday after his death. I was meditating on the incredible sacrifice Jesus made on my behalf. The Spirit began to emphasize how Jesus forgave those who crucified Him, and the words that the Holy Spirit highlighted to me were the words spoken by Jesus, "Father forgive them for they know not what they are doing" (Luke 23:34). Immediately the Spirit gave me the words Stephen spoke as he was being stoned to death and prayed, "Lord do not hold this sin against them" (Acts 7:59–60). I suddenly realized the Holy Spirit, which I sometimes call a baptism in love, was taking me to a whole new level of forgiveness. It was because of the baptism in the Holy Spirit that I was able to hear and receive such truth. The same Holy Spirit that was in Stephen, causing him to pray such a prayer, was also in me.

I instantly began to pray that God would not hold anything against Dad for that which he committed and omitted to do. I pleaded earnestly for nothing ever to be held against him for all the things he said and did to me, and also for never telling me, "I love you," which I longed to hear just once. I began to plead, "God, please do not hold this against him because I do not want to see him go to hell." I knew the Bible says, "If you forgive anyone his sins, they are forgiven; if you do not forgive them, they are not forgiven" (John 20:23 NIV). Jesus also says, "I tell you the truth, whatever you bind on earth will be bound in heaven, and whatever you loose on earth will be loosed in heaven" (Matt. 18:18 NIV). What serious words. This verse gave me a burden for my dad, and I did not want to be responsible for anything to be held against him.

This encounter with the Holy Spirit changed my entire view on forgiveness, no matter who it is or what they did to me. "If I do not forgive, I will not be forgiven" makes forgiveness a salvation issue. If you are wondering how to forgive someone who has died or refuses to be reconciled with you, pray the prayer of Stephen: "Father, do not hold this sin against them." When praying that prayer from the heart, the matter is settled and done.

God does not want us to live in condemnation and guilt. So do not carry that heavy burden. If someone holds a grudge against you, do your best to make it right. They may choose not to talk and make peace with you. If they refuse to reconcile after you have made an effort, it is their problem. We forgive another who has died or will not speak with us by asking God to not hold the sin against them because they do not know what they are doing. If you forgive with a sincere heart, it is finished.

Dads, do not call your children stupid, worthless, not amounting to anything, or degrade them in any way; and never use profanity in disciplining your children. If you have done such things, apologize to them and tell them you love them. As a parent, I understand how difficult some situations are. I know how easy it is to lose it with them. Always tell your kids you love them. Correction is necessary, but your words need to be out of compassion for their good.

There is one other area of forgiveness, and that is to forgive yourself. Do you feel guilty or carry a burden concerning something you did or did not do? Jesus took our guilt as well as our guiltiness upon Himself on the Cross. Holding on to guilt after receiving Christ is one of Satan's strategies to hinder us in our walk with the Lord. He likes to mess us up and make us ineffective in walking in the Spirit. If Christ has set you free, you are free indeed. You are His child, adopted into His family, and He loves you deeply. He has dressed you in clothes of His righteousness.

You are royalty, His son or daughter. He rejoices over you with singing. Believe it. Don't fall for Satan's lies.

If you forgive yourself and those who have wronged you, you will have unloaded a heavy burden. Not forgiving someone is a heavy burden that affects you and your effectiveness in the kingdom. But the real seriousness of not forgiving is that you will not receive forgiveness from the Father in heaven.

> "For if you forgive men when they sin against you, your heavenly Father will also forgive you. But if you do not forgive men their sins, your Father will not forgive your sins" (Matt. 6:14, 15).

Questions for discussion:

1.   Is there anyone in your life, when you think of them, that sets off a high-octane ping inside you?
2.   If there is anyone in your life who has wounded you in word or deed, have you forgiven them?
3.   What is the most serious consequence of not forgiving someone?
4.   Do you have any regrets in your life? Have you forgiven yourself?
5.   How do you forgive someone who hurt you and has died?

CHAPTER 8

WATER BAPTISM

〜◦〜

Jesus said, "Whoever believes and is baptized will be saved" (Mark 16:16).

There is probably no other topic in Christianity with as much uncertainty and confusion as water baptism. There is confusion over why, when, how, to whom, and by whom involving the administration of this sacrament. Is water baptism necessary for salvation? Or, is water baptism merely an outward act representing an inward experience? People have asked many questions like where does baptism fit into the covenants, and so forth. Throughout church history, there has been much change and division in the practice of baptism. Many opinions have been published, adding to the mix-up. This confusion should not be too surprising when we comprehend the significance of baptism and understand the battle in the heavenly realms against baptism. Satan and the powers of darkness have been having a heyday with this one.

Baptism has confused and split various people groups over differing thoughts. All of this confusion has originated with people influenced by the powers of darkness and not by God. God intended water baptism to unify the body, not to divide it. It was designed to make us all one, one body in Christ, even Jew and Gentile. Listen to Paul in the Word of God: "And all who have been united with Christ in baptism have put on Christ, like putting on new clothes. There is no longer Jew or Gentile, slave or free, male and female. For you are all one in Christ Jesus" (Gal. 3:27–28; NLT).

There is already a significant move by the Holy Spirit to unify the body in baptism, and this move will only increase as the day of His appearing approaches—and likewise the opposition. The Holy Spirit will restore baptism in the bride to its original intent by God as taught by the apostles. As we proceed, we need to use Scripture only, not all the extra-scriptural verses taken out of context, but Scripture about Christian baptism in the new covenant. This study may require unlearning previous thoughts. And, it is very difficult to unlearn beliefs that have been set in our heads for a long time. We need to recognize that culture and tradition are powerful and often deceptive forces at work in all of us. It requires the help of the Holy Spirit to change a mindset because it is a stronghold, a religious and traditional one at that.

Baptism has been a struggle for me as well as for many others. I was brought up and still attend a church in a denomination that practices infant baptism. I heard a lot of sermons on infant baptism, none of which I could verify in Scripture. Many assumptions used to justify this practice are unbiblical. After surrendering my life to Christ, I knew for sure in my heart that I needed to be baptized. So I asked several pastors to baptize me, and all refused for fear of what the denomination would do to them.

However, if I would go along on a church tour to Israel, they would be willing to baptize me in the Jordan River, which others in our church did. In Scripture, it did not matter in which body of water a person was baptized. To be baptized again after being "baptized" as an infant was considered to be a great sin, even unforgivable. I was told I would be undoing what my parents did for me, to which I had no response at the time. However, later the Spirit said, "I would be completing what my parents did for me in their promise to raise me according to God's Word." There was a bondage of fear put on the laity as far as "rebaptism" is concerned.

As I studied Scripture, I made a list of all the verses in the New Testament concerning baptism in the cover of my Bible, as I did with many other topics. It was like making my own concordance. The practice was of great value, even to this day. It gave me a clear understanding and was used by the Holy Spirit to lead and guide me into all truth. Even though I heard many sermons on infant baptism, I never heard one sermon on believer's baptism to this day. It was actually the sermons on infant baptism that convinced me of the error. I knew what the Bible said concerning water baptism.

In my heart, I knew I needed to be baptized. But, how would I accomplish that when no pastor would baptize me? God had an interesting way of solving the problem. A young man asked me to mentor him, which I did. After some time, he came to me asking me to baptize him. I thought, wow, what do I do with that? I was not ordained as a minister of Word and Sacrament, which I always assumed was a requirement. As I began asking the Lord what to do with this, the Holy Spirit spoke to me, saying, "If you disciple someone, you must baptize that person." Immediately, the Holy Spirit brought to mind the Great Commission. I grabbed my Bible and opened it to Matthew 28. It was right there and overlooked all these years, saying, "Therefore, go and make disciples of all nations, baptizing them in the name of the Father, and the Son and the Holy Spirit." I could not believe how I read over it many times and never saw it that way. Make disciples, baptizing them! All of us have the command to make disciples. I realized there is nothing in Scripture about being ordained to baptize someone. Certainly, ordained people should do baptisms, but it is not limited to them only. If you are so committed to making disciples, you should baptize, also freeing preachers to focus on preaching the Word. Watch the Scripture coming up, and you will see the pattern.

At the same time, my mentee led another person to the Lord who requested baptism. Since my mentee was attending a house church, he asked me to ask my pastor if he would baptize this guy. Since he was not baptized as an infant, indeed, they would baptize him, but he had to first appear before the elders to answer questions. This guy had never been in a church, so he was terrified to come into a church, let alone answer questions before the elders. He was too scared to do that, and therefore, he was refused baptism.

It was at that time the Holy Spirit spoke to me, saying, "It is a serious sin to refuse baptism to anyone who requests baptism." So, with a large-sized group, we went down to the river, where he wanted to be baptized. We heard his testimony, and many tears were shed as he shared his story and was baptized. After baptism, we all gathered around him and had a time of prayer over him. He was a real babe in Christ but became a follower of Jesus through discipleship and teaching.

After the two encounters with the Holy Spirit, I knew I had to baptize my mentee, and I had not yet been baptized myself. Since no pastor would baptize me, I also gained knowledge that I could have one baptize me who mentored me. I asked a person who had mentored me many years ago to baptize me, which he joyfully did. I proclaimed the message at my baptism using every verse concerning baptism in the New Testament. At my baptism, I said, "Knowing what the scriptures say, I will not go to the grave nor meet the Lord in the air without being baptized." With friends and family gathered around, I went under for Jesus at

Sandy Hollow, a body of water east of Sioux Center. I experienced great joy, knowing that after forty-three years of coming into a relationship with Jesus that I was finally set free to follow Jesus in water baptism. I was set free to be obedient, to bury the old dead nature and to rise with Him in the resurrected life. As I publicly identified with Jesus, I was also clothed with Christ as I was enveloped in the water. Baptism is an expression of love for Jesus, being united with Him in intimacy. Who would not desire such a relationship? Do you altogether prefer Him? Are you, personally, willing to obey?

There are ways to arrive at whatever we want the Bible to say. Scriptures are taken out of context so they can be twisted to say what people desire the Bible to say. Also, using Scripture, which has nothing to do with the topic at hand, is used and then applied as one wishes. Failure to use *all* scriptures on a given topic to avoid a contradiction and trying to support a particular belief is another error. False premises produce false teachings. Using the wrong set of assumptions also enables you to prove whatever you like. Many like to use the Old Testament in developing their belief system on baptism, which leads to false premises, arriving at wrong conclusions. However, Christian baptism is only practiced and taught in the New Testament. Therefore, let us consider all Scripture in the New Testament in our quest for truth, not just some of them.

1. Jesus, Our Example

We begin with Jesus as He approached John the Baptist, who was preparing the way for Jesus and baptizing for repentance of sins. Jesus asked John to baptize Him, and John tried to deter Jesus, saying I am the one who needs to be baptized by you. But Jesus replied:

Let it be so now; it is proper for us to do this to fulfill all righteousness. Then John consented. As soon as Jesus was baptized, He went up out of the water. At that moment, heaven was opened, and he saw the Spirit of God descending like a dove and lighting on him. And a voice from heaven said, "This is my Son, whom I love; with him, I am well pleased. (Matt. 3:15–17; NIV)

Jesus, being our example, personally submitted to water baptism and insisted on being baptized. Jesus said that it was proper for Him to be baptized. Jesus, being without sin, did not need to be baptized for the forgiveness of sins as all others. Jesus said, His baptism was to fulfill all righteousness. If Jesus, the Son of God, needed to be baptized to do what was right in the Father's sight, then yes, I also needed to submit to baptism personally. Without any doubt, God the Father approved of this act of obedience as He said in verse 17: "This is my Son, whom I love; with Him, I am well pleased." Notice that immediately, heaven opened, and the Holy Spirit descended on Jesus! Have you personally submitted to baptism, even insisting on it as Jesus did? If Jesus needed to submit to baptism to fulfill all righteousness, should we not also need to do likewise?

2. The Great Commission

Next, consider the Great Commission given by Jesus as recorded in Matthew and Mark:

All authority in heaven and on earth has been given to me. Therefore go and make disciples of all nations, baptizing them in the name of the Father

and of the Son and the Holy Spirit, and teaching
them to obey everything I have commanded you.
And surely I am with you always, to the very end
of the age. (Matt. 28:18–20; NIV)

He said to them, "Go into all the world and preach
the good news to all creation. Whoever believes
and is baptized will be saved, but whoever does not
believe will be condemned. (Mark16:15–16; NIV)

In the Matthew passage, baptizing people is part of making disciples, just as teaching them to obey all things Jesus commanded. A person must become a believer before one can become a disciple and be baptized. It is impossible to disciple infants because they are not capable of discipleship. Therefore, baptism is part of becoming a disciple and is for believers. In this passage, the people who are making disciples out of others are to perform the baptism. That is the way Jesus, as well as other followers of Jesus, did the baptisms. The quote of Jesus in the gospel of Mark, "whoever believes and is baptized will be saved," should be enough to settle all debates and questions concerning baptism. In no way can this statement be interpreted that someone else can do it for you, like your parents. Both believing and being baptized must be a personal decision.

In the passage recorded by Mark, it says, "those who believe and are baptized will be saved." The conjunction *and* is significant because it joins the two, requiring both to be done by anyone desiring to come to Christ. This passage in no way implies that someone can believe for you and get you baptized. The new covenant is personal. A person must personally believe and personally be baptized into Christ Jesus in the name of the Father, the Son, and the Holy Spirit. No one can do either for you. The conjunction *and* means if you need to do the one, you need to do the other as well. I know the "yah, buts" in the reasoning of man, but we need to read the Bible for what it says, even if it differs from our culture and tradition.

3. Who Does the Baptizing?

"The Pharisees heard that Jesus was gaining and baptizing more disciples than John, although, in fact, it was not Jesus who baptized, but his disciples" (John 4:1–2, NIV). Jesus had His disciples do the actual baptizing, rather than doing it Himself. Jesus was busy ministering. His disciples were very ordinary, socially low people, and far from being approved by the religious establishment for ordination. In the Great Commission, quoted above, the one who disciples is to baptize and teach obedience. Jesus had no requirements of special ordination to perform the baptism as our culture does. What was so important was the heart of the one being baptized.

As we go on through the New Testament, take note of who does the baptizing. Phillip, not one of the twelve, but an ordained deacon, baptized the Ethiopian eunuch (Acts 8:38). Paul, likewise, led many to Christ but only baptized a few of them (1 Cor. 1:17). The ones Paul was making into disciples had to be doing the baptizing. And, who baptized Paul? Most likely, Ananias did.

4. Peter Explained Baptism

The book of Acts is the most comprehensive book on evangelism in the Bible. It lays out the steps to a proper initiation into the body of Christ. Peter's very first sermon, highly anointed, as he had just been baptized in the Holy Spirit, says, "Each one needs to be baptized" (Acts 2:38 NIV). *Each one,* again, makes baptism personal. His words were full of power to convict and convince people of their need for Jesus. The baptism in the Holy Spirit is for power in your words and your deeds. Peter explains that what they were seeing and hearing was the outpouring of the Spirit as prophesied in the book of Joel. Peter preached that Christ was crucified, died, was buried, rose from the grave, ascended into heaven, and is seated at the right hand of the Father, sending the Holy Spirit. The response of the people to an intense conviction was, "What shall we do?"

> When the people heard this, they were cut to the heart [with remorse and anxiety], and they said to Peter and the rest of the apostles, "Brothers, what shall we do?" And Peter said to them, "Repent [change your old way of thinking, turn from your sinful ways, accept and follow Jesus the Messiah] and be baptized, each one of you, in the name of Jesus Christ because of the forgiveness of your sins; and you will receive the gift of the Holy Spirit. For the promise [of the Holy Spirit] is for you and your children and for all who are far away [including the Gentiles], as many as the Lord our God calls to Himself." (Acts 2:38–39; AMP)

Peter went on preaching, urging people to repent, and all who believed and received his message were baptized, adding about 3,000 souls to the body of believers. Notice the order in the steps of initiation into Christ Jesus of repenting and turning to Jesus, and then submitting to baptism. After that, they were to go on and receive the baptism in the Holy Spirit. It is stated very clearly in the Word of God. How could we get it so messed up?

5. The Promise to You and Your Children

First, in the same passage of Acts 2:38–39, "the promise is to you and your children," is not about water baptism, an error in reading, but about the baptism in the Holy Spirit. "The promise," is always the promised Holy Spirit as received at Pentecost. And the second error in reading the above passage is the word *children* taken out of context and used as *infants*. The Word translated *children* means descendants born to a person, not infants. I am a child and always will be a child of my parents, regardless of my age. Without all the detail, a different Greek word would be required to mean infants.

As the church, we are to be united in baptism; however, we are not joined in mind and thought on baptism, which has become divisive in the body of Christ. It is often said, "It is healthy to have differing opinions about baptism," but that allows the evil one to cause division in the body.

> I appeal to you, brothers, in the name of our Lord Jesus Christ, that all of you agree with one another so that there may be no divisions among you and that you may be perfectly united in mind and thought. (1 Cor. 1:10; NIV)

> Is Christ divided? Was Paul crucified for you? Were you baptized into the name of Paul? I am thankful that I did not baptize any of you except Crispus and Gaius, so no one can say that you were baptized into my name. (Yes, I also baptized the household of Stephanas; beyond that, I don't remember if I baptized anyone else.) For Christ did not send me to baptize, but to preach the gospel—not with

words of human wisdom, lest the cross of Christ
be emptied of its power. (1 Cor. 1:13–17; NIV)

6. Believe First, Then Submit to Baptism

Many were converted under Paul's preaching, and from
Scripture, Paul insisted on baptism after believing. Therefore,
since he only baptized a few, he had others perform the baptisms
as Jesus did. Paul was following his calling and using his gifts to
spread the gospel as far as possible. In Galatians, Paul writes the
following:

You are all sons of God through faith in Christ
Jesus. For all of you who were baptized into Christ
have clothed yourselves with Christ. There is neither Jew nor Greek, slave nor free, male nor female,
for you are all one in Christ Jesus. If you belong
to Christ, then you are Abraham's seed, and heirs
according to the promise. (Gal. 3:26–29; NIV)

Take note that faith in Christ Jesus precedes baptism as in
all of the New Covenant. As we are clothed with the water in
baptism, we need to receive the covering of Christ Jesus when
receiving water baptism and becoming one in the body of Christ.
In believing and baptism into Christ, we become one in His body,
the church, and become heirs according to the promise.

Continuing in the book of Acts, we see more baptisms. When
the believers were persecuted, they were scattered throughout
Judea and Samaria. Philip, one of the deacons, went down to a
city in Samaria, preaching the Word of God as did others who
were scattered. Miracles and signs followed Philip's preaching.
Demons were cast out, and many were healed, resulting in great

joy in that city. "But when they believed Philip as he preached the good news of the kingdom of God and the name of Jesus Christ, they were baptized, both men and women" (Acts 8:12; NIV).

People again believed and were baptized after believing the good news. Later, the angel of the Lord instructed Philip to go to Gaza. While on the road, Philip met an Ethiopian eunuch who had gone to Jerusalem to worship and was on his way home. While sitting in his chariot, he was reading from the book of Isaiah. Philip approached the chariot and began conversing with the man and sharing the scriptures with him.

> The eunuch asked Philip, 'tell me, please, who is the prophet talking about, himself or someone else?' Then Philip began with that very passage of Scripture and told him the good news about Jesus. As they traveled along the road, they came to some water, and the eunuch said, 'Look here is water. Why shouldn't I be baptized?' And he gave orders to stop the chariot. Then both Philip and the eunuch went down into the water, and Philip baptized him. When they came up out of the water, the Spirit of the Lord suddenly took Philip away, and the eunuch did not see him again. (Acts 8:34–39; NIV)

It is evident that Philip told the eunuch the good news about receiving Jesus and baptism, or he would not have known about baptism. The eunuch believed first and then was baptized. The baptism was immersion as they went down into the water and up out of the water. In this case, the baptizer was an ordained deacon, not an ordained minister of Word and Sacrament.

In Acts 9, we read of Saul's conversion, his healing, being filled with the Holy Spirit, and baptized. After Saul's encounter with Jesus on the road to Damascus, he was blind, did not eat or drink anything for three days. Saul and a man named Ananias both had a vision for Ananias to minister to Saul and that he might restore his eyesight.

> Then Ananias went to the house and entered it. Placing his hands on Saul, he said, "Brother Saul, the Lord—Jesus who appeared to you on the road as you were coming here—has sent me so that you may see again and be filled with the Holy Spirit." Immediately, something like scales fell from Saul's eyes, and he could see again. He got up and was baptized, and after taking some food, he regained his strength. (Acts 9:17–18; NIV)

The entire story is theatrical, but for now, we only look at Saul's baptism. Again, Saul believed, and then baptism followed believing, as this is consistent throughout Scripture. From the context, most likely, Ananias baptized Saul.

7. Gentiles Are Baptized

In Acts chapter 10, we have the story of Cornelius and the Gentiles receiving salvation, Spirit baptism, and water baptism. How can I, as a Gentile, not love this story? After two supernatural visions, one to Peter and one to Cornelius, Peter went to the household of Cornelius and began to share the gospel. Peter explained that everyone who believes in Jesus receives forgiveness of sins through His name. To the astonishment of all present, including the Jews, the Holy Spirit was poured out on Gentiles.

> While Peter was still speaking these words, the
> Holy Spirit came on all who heard the message.
> The circumcised believers who had come with
> Peter were astonished that the gift of the Holy
> Spirit had been poured out even on the Gentiles.
> For they heard them speaking in tongues and
> praising God. Then Peter said, "Can anyone keep
> these people from being baptized with water? They
> have received the Holy Spirit just as we have." So
> he ordered that they be baptized in the name of
> Jesus Christ. (Acts 10:44–48; NIV)

The Bible explains that Cornelius had invited relatives and close friends, a large gathering of people to hear what Peter has to say. Notice that the pattern of water baptism and then Spirit baptism is reversed in this story. They received the baptism in the Holy Spirit as they believed Peter's message, convincing the circumcised believers that water baptism was for the Gentiles also. God demonstrated that salvation, water baptism, and Spirit baptism is for everyone who believes regardless if they are Jew or Gentile, for we are all one, baptized into Christ. In Acts chapter 11, Peter needed to explain his actions in visiting Gentiles. He told how Cornelius heard in his vision that Peter would say how he and his household would be saved. So Cornelius invited a large group of people to listen to the good news. It is incredible what God did in this story.

> Peter was defending his actions saying, "As I
> began to speak, the Holy Spirit came on them
> as he had come on us at the beginning. Then I
> remembered what the Lord had said: 'John bap-
> tized with water, but you will be baptized with the

Holy Spirit. So if God gave them the same gift as he gave us, who believed in the Lord Jesus Christ, who was I to think that I could oppose God?" (Acts 11:15–17; NIV)

How many of us oppose God by refusing water baptism for some man-made reason? How many oppose the words of Jesus, who said, "You will be baptized in the Holy Spirit?" Many oppose the language of baptism in the Holy Spirit because of the misunderstood wording and incorrect teaching of the "one baptism" in Ephesians 4. There is clearly a difference between Spirit and water baptism. The two are different and did not happen simultaneously.

8. The Whole Household

In Acts chapters 16 to 18, we encounter entire households being baptized. The word *household* is often used to justify baptizing infants because someone in the house may have been a baby. Even though the probability of that happening is slim, we need to check it out with Scripture. There is no mention of infants in the three household baptisms in these three chapters, and therefore, it is very presumptuous to say it included the baptism of infants. But, there is a more substantial reason why infants are not included here. Most importantly, notice, reading in context, all who were baptized believed first. Consequently, we still have a believer's baptism.

The first example is in Acts 16:14–15 NIV, where Lydia and her household were baptized. Verse 15 states, "One of those listening was a woman named Lydia, a dealer in purple cloth from the city of Thyatira, who was a worshiper of God. The Lord opened her heart to respond to Paul's message. When she and the members of her household were baptized, she invited us to her home."

The Lord opened her heart, and she responded to Paul's message meaning that she believed, and then she was baptized.

The next example is in the same chapter, verses 25–34, as Paul and Silas were in prison. Beginning at verse 29:

> The jailer called for lights, rushed in and fell trembling before Paul and Silas. He then brought them out and asked, "Sirs, what must I do to be saved?" They replied, "Believe in the Lord Jesus, and you will be saved—you and your household." Then they spoke the word of the Lord to him and to all the others in his house. At that hour of the night, the jailer took them and washed their wounds; then immediately, he and all his family were baptized. The jailer brought them into his house and set a meal before them; he was filled with joy because he had come to believe in God—he and his whole family."

Paul and Silas first spoke the Word of the Lord to the entire household, and he and his whole family and servants believed in God. Everyone capable of accepting the message believed in God and was baptized. Since all who were baptized, believed first, it is evident that the whole household has nothing to do with infants because they all believed.

The next passage where the entire household was baptized is in Acts 18:7–8: "Then Paul left the synagogue and went next door to the house of Titus Justus, a worshiper of God. Crispus, the synagogue ruler, and his entire household believed in the Lord, and many of the Corinthians who heard him believed and were baptized." Take note that others besides the household, other Corinthians, also believed and were baptized. Many excuses are manufactured, but in Scripture, it is always believing first, then baptism when reading the entire story.

9. Rebaptism

Chapter 18 ends with an exciting story about Apollos coming to Ephesus. Apollos was highly educated and a skilled orator. No one could stand against him as he was fully knowledgeable of the Scriptures and Jesus. He knew what John the Baptist preached and also taught the baptism of John the Baptist, a baptism unto repentance. Now it happened that Aquila and Priscilla were listening to the bold preaching of Apollos. Realizing that Apollos did not have complete knowledge of Jesus, they invited Apollos to their home and "explained to him the way of God more adequately" (verse 26). It is impressive that Apollos, a brilliant and gifted man, would listen to two tentmakers. Apollos was also very humble, willing to be taught, despite his superior education. Are we today ready to receive information more adequately by listening to God's Word and the Holy Spirit who leads and guides us into all truth?

Paul came to Ephesus in chapter 19. The story of Apollos is such a setup for what happens next. Paul began asking questions. In reality, he was asking, if you did not receive the baptism in the Holy Spirit, then what baptism did you receive? They responded, "John's baptism." John's baptism was a water baptism of repentance for the forgiveness of sins. Paul went on to explain that John the Baptist also preached Jesus, who was coming after him and to follow Jesus, who Paul was also teaching. "On hearing this, they were baptized into the name of the Lord Jesus. When Paul placed his hands on them, the Holy Spirit came on them, and they spoke in tongues and prophesied" (Acts 19:5–6; NIV).

They were initially baptized in water for the forgiveness of sin only, but not including new life in Christ. As Apollos needed to have the way of God through baptism into Jesus explained more adequately, so did the Ephesians need to have an adequate explanation of baptism. Therefore, they were baptized again into the name of the Lord Jesus. Some look on rebaptism as a sin, undoing what was done as an infant. An infant is not capable of submitting to baptism, repenting of sins, burying the old, and rising to a new life in Christ, as explained in the New Testament. Rebaptism is not undoing anything but being obedient in following Jesus, fulfilling what was done by the parent's promise. I needed "a more adequate" explanation of baptism; therefore, I was baptized, personally submitting and identifying with Jesus's death and resurrection, as explained in Romans 6, and I will rise with Him, as promised.

The entire book of Acts teaches that first, we need to repent of our sins; second, we need to receive Jesus or to believe in Him; third, we need to be baptized in water, and fourth, go on to be baptized in the Holy Spirit. That is the order in which it usually occurs, with one exception, which was the Gentiles in chapter 10. The reason for that is, first, the apostles had to see that the Lord accepted the Gentiles just as He accepted the Jews by giving Gentiles the Holy Spirit in the same way as the Jews received the Holy Spirit in the beginning. Then Peter was willing to baptize them in water also. The book of Acts shows us how to evangelize, giving us the proper way to initiate people into the kingdom. The epistles give us an additional explanation of the significance and importance of water baptism.

10. Paul to the Romans on Baptism

In the early chapters of Romans, Paul explains the sinfulness of man, the wrath of God toward sin, God's righteous judgment, the faithfulness of God toward humankind, God's forgiveness through faith in Jesus alone, and all that Christ accomplished for us by His grace. In Romans 6, he details dying to sin and rising to a new life in Christ Jesus when we are baptized in water. Romans 6 is an excellent passage showing us what should happen when we are baptized. Baptism is not merely a symbol. The Bible says: "Or don't you know that all of us who were baptized into Christ Jesus were baptized into his death? We were therefore buried with him through baptism into death so that just as Christ was raised from the dead through the glory of the Father, we too may live a new life" (Rom. 6:3–4; NIV).

It is interesting to read this passage in the NLT, which reads joined with Christ in baptism rather than baptized into Christ. That is what the preposition *into* means. In Christian baptism, we identify with Christ and are united with Christ in His crucifixion (death), burial, and resurrection. We die to the old nature, our old self; we crucify it; we are freed from sin; we bury it in the water of baptism; and as we come up out of the water, we are raised to a new life in Christ. We leave our old sin nature behind in the grave. Did you leave it behind when you were baptized? Did your baptism mean that to you? Like the Ephesians, when things are explained "more adequately," people get baptized again. Merely going through the motions is not adequate. Let the Spirit lead and guide you into all truth. In the Bible, it is undoubtedly not sinning, as some say, "to be baptized again is sin." That is a lie from the enemy. You are not undoing anything but are fully committing yourself to Christ and following Him in obedience.

If we have been united with him like this in his death, we will certainly also be united with him in his resurrection. For we know that our old self was crucified with him so that the body of sin might be done away with, that we should no longer be slaves to sin—because anyone who has died has been freed from sin. Now if we died with Christ, we believe that we will also live with him. For we know that since Christ was raised from the dead, he cannot die again; death no longer has mastery over him. The death he died, he died to sin once for all; but the life he lives he lives to God. (Rom. 6:5–10; NIV)

If we died with Christ, we would be raised with Christ. Is not that the most exciting thing anyone can imagine? Those who have submitted to baptism into Christ will be raised when Jesus returns. That is what Jesus meant when he said, "Those who believe and are baptized will be saved." It will be crucial on judgment day. Yes, I know the thief on the cross wasn't baptized; he was dying, but all those who are able and understand God's Word must be baptized. The Word is clear. Those who obey are the ones who love Him. Do you love Him with all your heart, soul, mind, and strength?

In baptism, we intentionally defeat sin and live for Christ. Scripture goes on to explain; we count ourselves dead to sin, so we are not to let sin reign in our bodies obeying its evil desires. We are now to reckon ourselves dead to sin and alive to God in Christ Jesus. So we are not to let sin reign in our mortal bodies, obeying its evil desires, because we are not under the law but under grace. Grace is the power to escape sin, not to continue in it as some teach. In baptism, we clothe ourselves with Christ, and his clothing is his righteousness. We are enveloped in Him in baptism. "You are all sons of God through faith in Christ Jesus, for all of you who were baptized into Christ have clothed yourselves with Christ" (Gal. 3:26–27; NIV).

11. One Baptism

As I mentioned earlier, there is much confusion over the "one baptism" in Ephesians 4:4–6 (NIV): "There is one body and one Spirit—just as you were called to one hope when you were called—one Lord, one faith, one baptism, one God and Father of all, who is over all and through all and in all." The context of this verse is on unity in the body, the unity of the Spirit. The word *one*, which is used several times in this passage is about the uniqueness of each subject. Some interpret "one" to mean "once," which cannot be for then all the "ones" mean "once." "One" is not the same as "once." If it is baptism once, then it is Lord once or faith once, and so on. Jesus is Lord all the time, and we live by constant faith, not just once. One baptism is used by some to imply that if you were baptized as an infant, then you must not be baptized again as a believer. If that is true, then it should not have been permitted in the Ephesian church in Acts 19, but Paul not only allowed it but encouraged it and is included in the inspired Word of God.

There is another reason in Scripture why this cannot be. Hebrews 6 speaks of more than one baptism:

> Therefore let us leave the elementary teachings about Christ and go on to maturity, not laying again the foundation of repentance from acts that lead to death, and of faith in God, instruction about baptisms, the laying on of hands, the resurrection of the dead, and eternal judgment. (Heb. 6:1–2; NIV)

Notice the "s" on the word baptism, reading *baptisms*, meaning more than one baptism. Reading Scripture carefully, we make the following observations concerning other baptisms. Pay careful attention to *who* is baptized; *in, into* or *with* what are you being baptized; and *by* whom are you baptized: "The body is a unit, though it is made up of many parts; and though all its parts are many, they form one body. So it is with Christ. For we were all baptized *by* one Spirit *into* one body—whether Jews or Greeks, slave or free—and we were all given one Spirit to drink" (1 Cor. 12:13).

This baptism is about *all* who have received Christ. They are all baptized into the one body of the one Lord. The one Spirit baptizes us. Notice how everything matches perfectly with the passage in Ephesians 4. First Corinthians 12:13 is the one baptism into the one body by the one Spirit. And, it is not water baptism. This baptism into the body occurs when we are born again or born of the Holy Spirit. Salvation is a work of the Spirit in that we are first called or drawn by the Spirit, then born of the Spirit, sanctified by the Spirit, and we will be raised by the Spirit when Jesus returns. The entire salvation process is the work of the *one* Spirit working over a whole lifetime, not just once.

The second baptism we will consider is baptism *in* water. After receiving Christ, *one*, as a believer, is baptized in water by another believer. We can see this in all the examples of water baptism we just looked at in the book of Acts, like the Ethiopian eunuch was baptized in water by Philip.

The third baptism mentioned in Scripture is the baptism in the Holy Spirit. *We*, as believers, are baptized *with* the Holy Spirit and fire by Jesus. It is mentioned in all four gospels by John the Baptist who said:

> I baptize with water for repentance. But after me will come one who is more powerful than I, whose sandals I am not fit to carry. He will baptize you with the Holy Spirit and with fire. His winnowing fork is in his hand, and he will clear his threshing floor, gathering his wheat into the barn

and burning up the chaff with unquenchable fire.
(Matt. 3:11–12; NIV)

There are two baptisms mentioned in these verses alone, water
baptism and Spirit baptism. John baptized with water, and Jesus
baptizes with the Holy Spirit. These verses cannot be explained,
nor understood, when all baptisms are incorrectly lumped together
to make up one baptism. The one baptism is then used to explain
away the baptism in the Holy Spirit, claiming there cannot be
another baptism. That is why some always use "filled with the
Holy Spirit" rather than "baptized in the Holy Spirit." But Jesus
used the expression, baptized in the Holy Spirit, as well as John
the Baptist and the apostles.

A fourth baptism mentioned in Scripture is the baptism of
suffering.

> But Jesus said unto them, "You don't know what
> you are asking! Are you able to drink from the bitter
> cup of suffering I am about to drink? Are you able
> to be baptized with the baptism of suffering I must
> be baptized with?" "Oh yes," they replied, "we
> are able!" Then Jesus told them, "You will indeed
> drink from my bitter cup and be baptized with my
> baptism of suffering." (Mark 10:38–39; NLT)

Jesus and his followers were baptized with suffering by unbelievers who lived in darkness. The suffering of Jesus was unimag-
inable. History declares that all the disciples died a martyr's death
except John. All were severely persecuted. Many in the world
today suffer significantly at the hands of people who live in darkness. False religions feel very threatened by Christianity. In reality,
it is the battle waged by the powers of wickedness in the heavenly

realms against the truth. The Bible says, "Those who live godly lives in Christ Jesus will be persecuted" (2 Tim. 3:12; NIV).

12. Baptism and Circumcision

There is a teaching that infant baptism replaces circumcision. There are two circumcisions mentioned in the Bible. They are the circumcision of the flesh, done by the hands of men, and the circumcision of the heart done by the Holy Spirit (Rom. 2:29). Now the circumcision of the flesh done on the eighth day after birth is the only circumcision that could be replaced by infant baptism. The circumcision of the heart happens when we are born again with the cutting away of the sinful nature, accomplished by the Spirit at the time of the new birth, and therefore does not occur in infancy. Colossians 2 is used to justify this teaching.

> So then, just as you received Christ Jesus as Lord, continue to live in him, rooted and built up in him, strengthened in the faith as you were taught, and overflowing with thankfulness.

> See to it that no one takes you captive through hollow and deceptive philosophy, which depends on human tradition and the basic principles of this world rather than on Christ.

> For in Christ, all the fullness of the Deity lives in bodily form, and you have been given fullness in Christ, who is the head over every power and authority. In him you were also circumcised, in the putting off of the sinful nature, not with a circumcision done by the hands of men but with the

circumcision done by Christ, having been buried with him in baptism and raised with him through your faith in the power of God, who raised him from the dead. (Col. 2:6–12; NIV)

This Scripture clearly states it is not the circumcision done by the hands of men.

At the beginning of these verses, verse 6, the context is at the time of receiving Christ. It is followed by a warning not to be taken in by hollow and deceptive philosophy based on human tradition, which has happened over the years. This passage says just the opposite of what some teach. It says, "not with the circumcision done by the hands of men (which is circumcision of infants), but with the circumcision done by Christ, having been buried with him in baptism." This Scripture shows the cutting off of the sinful nature at the baptism of one who has received Christ, which is spiritual circumcision and not physical circumcision. We are raised with Him through faith in the power of God. These verses fully support believer's baptism that coincides perfectly with Romans 6.

13. Baptism and Salvation

There is one more passage in the New Testament on baptism that needs to be considered. Speaking of the flood, resulting in the salvation of Noah and his family, the Bible states:

In it (the flood), only a few people, eight in all, were saved through water, and this water (flood-water) symbolizes baptism that now saves you also—not the removal of dirt from the body but the pledge of a good conscience toward God. It saves you by the resurrection of Jesus Christ, who has gone into heaven and is at God's right hand—with angels, authorities, and powers in submission to him. (1 Pet. 3:20–21; NIV)

The floodwater symbolizes baptism, not the other way around, where baptism symbolizes the floodwater. Baptism is much more than a symbol. Baptism does much more than symbolize the washing away of sins. Your sins are washed away in baptism if you are doing as scripture instructs. The Bible says, "As the floodwaters saved Noah's family in the ark, likewise baptism saves us." Then it tells us how it saves us. It is not the water; it saves us by the pledge or appeal toward God through the resurrection of Jesus Christ and your identification with Christ's death, burial, and resurrection. In Romans 6, it says, "If we have been united with him like this in His death, we will certainly also be united with Him in His resurrection." It doesn't save us by the washing of the water. In baptism, we are also making a pledge or a response to God from a clean conscience. "If we died with Him, we will also live with Him!" That is how baptism saves us—by the resurrection. Jesus said, "Those who believe and are baptized will be saved," which means the same thing.

There is a critical link between baptism and salvation. It is by grace through faith that we are saved. But remember, the Bible explains, "Faith without works is dead or is not faith at all." Baptism is a personal response in faith of what Jesus accomplished on the Cross by His death and His resurrection. Personally submitting to baptism is the response or action we take demonstrating our faith. We obediently follow His command and example.

Infant baptism places high confidence in what man does since nothing has taken place in the infant's heart at this point. In some denominations, the baby is said to be saved when baptized. In other faiths, the baby is sealed by the Holy Spirit when baptized, which is the same as being saved because the indwelling Holy Spirit is our assurance of salvation with Christ in us. The Bible says:

> And you also were included in Christ when you heard the message of truth, the gospel of salvation. *Having believed,* you were marked in him with a seal, the promised Holy Spirit who is a deposit guaranteeing our inheritance until the redemption of those who are God's possession—to the praise of his glory. (Eph. 1:13–14; NIV my emphasis)

It is when you believe that you are marked with the seal, the promised Holy Spirit. Receiving Christ is impossible for an infant since they cannot hear the Word of truth nor comprehend the gospel of salvation. Infant baptism puts full confidence in what man does, the clergy, and nothing in what the person being baptized does. Also, take notice, "the promised Holy Spirit" is the seal that marks us. The seal is consistent with the Pentecostal experience in Acts 1 and 2 and other places in Scripture referring to the baptism in the Holy Spirit. According to this passage, you are sealed when you receive the promised Holy Spirit. This description is the same as receiving the Holy Spirit on the day of Pentecost.

In infant baptism, the inclusion of the parents promising to bring up the infant in the ways of the Lord is where the power lies. That part of infant baptism is good and is the same as infant dedication. Scripturally, it just should not be called baptism. The baby is not personally receiving baptism, which is what Jesus meant when He said, "those who believe and are baptized will be saved." His words do not express nor can be interpreted to indicate if someone else believes for you and submits to baptism for you, that you will be saved.

Infant baptism is very deceptive to many who have been baptized that way. It leads people to believe there is nothing else needed. It's all automatic from here on to the end, and those so baptized falsely think, "I'm on my way to heaven. I do not have to surrender my life to the Lord." It is followed by teaching, which lacks the instruction that you must be born again and die to self, which is assumed to have happened when you were baptized as a baby. Instead, it is followed by many dos and don'ts, following the law, which does not save. The belief is that I'm "good to go" since my parents had me baptized, I completed the requirements of my denomination, and I lived the best I could. Therefore, I'm saved. However, the most severe error associated with infant baptism is not permitting one to submit to baptism when becoming a believer. That is preventing one from obediently following Jesus.

There are questions I have asked, and you may also have some. What happened to my dad and mom, or others baptized as an infant, and never submitted to believers baptism? That is a good and is a fair question to ask. There are many other things to consider, in addition to water baptism. Most importantly, what kind of relationship did my parents have with Jesus? The answer to that is accompanied by much confusion. For many, it is what kind of a religious life did one live? Did they attend church most of the time? Did they walk the talk? Did they know the catechism? Did they obey the Ten Commandments? The list goes on and on. Baptism, in itself, does not save. Each one must also believe.

In reading Scripture, the real test is, will Jesus say on judgment day, "Depart from me for I do not know you?" It is not what we know about Him, but do we know Him? The difference is vast. To know Him, you need a deep personal relationship with Him, a bond of intimacy, and a loving relationship with others. Does the person love enough to follow and obey? Have they ever become a new creature in Christ Jesus? Have they died to sin? What was in the heart is the real issue. Their knowledge of baptism was not adequate. So I say, only God knows the heart, and He is the only one capable of such judgment, and that goes for those who have submitted to believer's baptism as well. Anyone can go through the motions without entering into a loving relationship and following the Lord.

I will share a testimony about my mother. When she was ninety years old and in a nursing home in Loveland, Colorado, we, her children and many grandchildren gathered to celebrate her birthday. They would allow her to go out of the nursing home under our supervision and care. On Sunday, I picked her up to go with us to church. During the service, I prayed, asking God to do something special for her on this special birthday. I sat next to her, observing her joy being in a worship service with her children. Near the end of the service, the pastor said that he felt led to celebrate the sacrament of communion. He requested a few people to go to the kitchen and prepare the elements.

Shortly, everything was ready. We were instructed to come to the front, taking a piece of bread, dipping it in the juice, and partaking. As we were in the front partaking of the sacrament, Mom suddenly exclaimed, "Oh, isn't this wonderful to celebrate Jesus together!" Immediately the Holy Spirit spoke to me, saying, "You will not partake of this together again until you eat and drink it anew in the kingdom." I shared this Word from the Spirit with the pastor after the service. He said that he felt led to have communion on the spot, and now he knew why. He said, "God loves you so much that He did that just for you." That took me back, but I believe He did it in answer to my request, and that He would also do that for any of His children.

I share that story with you because my mother was brought up in the same denomination as I was. It has been that way for generations. Therefore, she was baptized as an infant as well. From that communion experience, coupled with the Word I received from the Spirit, I believe I have assurance from the Spirit that she will be in heaven with me. She was very devoted and had a deep love relationship with the Lord. She was not adequately instructed in baptism, and I believe God's grace is sufficient to cover that omission, provided Jesus was in her heart. I do not think that is an excuse to refuse baptism nor to dismiss it. But, she did miss out on all the benefits of following Jesus in baptism. If you know what the Bible says about baptism, and if you love the Lord, you will submit to baptism out of love and obedient faith. There is so much grace going on in personally submitting to baptism and in taking a public stand in identifying yourself with Jesus. Following Jesus out of love is joyful and the ultimate expression of gratitude.

Another big question that is often asked is, "what happens to a baby or child who dies without being baptized?" I love the story of David and Bathsheba in 2 Samuel 12. David prayed and fasted for his infant son, who later died. David said, "Can I bring him back again? I will go to him, but he will not return to me." This story teaches that the child is in heaven, despite David's sin of adultery and murder. I also like the Scripture in 1 Corinthians 7:14, which explains that if one of the parents is a believer that the child is holy to God. Children go to heaven when they die. I also believe that aborted and miscarried children are in heaven. Praise God for His gracious promises.

Here is a summary of what the Bible says about Christian (believers) baptism.

1. You fulfill all righteousness, all God's requirements. (See Matt. 3:15.)
2. Being made a disciple as commanded in the Great Commission. (See Matt. 28:19.)
3. Believing and baptism result in salvation. (See Mark 16:16.)

4. For the forgiveness and washing away of sins. (See Acts 2:38; 22:16.)
5. We die to sin and bury the old nature. (See Rom. 6:2–4.)
6. We rise to a new life in Christ. (See Rom. 6:2–4.)
7. We are united with Christ in His resurrection. (See Rom. 6:5.)
8. We crucify the old self doing away with the body of sin and are no longer slaves to sin. (See Rom. 6:6.)
9. We now live with Christ. (See Rom. 6:8.)
10. We go from death to life. (See Rom. 6:13.)
11. We are united and clothed with Christ; His clothing is His righteousness. (See Gal. 3:27.)
12. We become complete through our union and identification with Christ. (See Col. 2:6–15.)
13. We receive the circumcision of Christ having the old nature cut off. (See Colossians 2:6–15.)
14. We are buried with Christ and raised to new life. (See Col. 2:6–15.)
15. We make a pledge or response to God from a clean conscience resulting in salvation. (See 1 Pet. 3:21.)

Some of these say the same thing in different words. However, it is interesting to see what all the verses say regarding baptism. Did your baptism mean that to you? If you are in a church that practices believer's baptism, you are fortunate, but, even in such a church, it can be done without proper understanding. Baptism is significant when done with full knowledge. I have never heard or been influenced by one sermon on believer's baptism to this day, but we all have many translations of the Bible to read for ourselves. Scripture has been my only influence. On my phone, I can quickly switch from one translation to another, gaining additional insight. Think of the advantage we have over older generations.

We have so much available today in studying God's Word. We are personally responsible for investigating the Scripture. We will have no excuses. Read your Bible for yourself.

Looking at the list above, seeing all the advantages and blessings in water baptism, who would not desire baptism? If you think, "I don't need to be baptized to go to heaven," you need to reconsider your relationship with the Lord. If you love Him, you will never see how much you can get by without doing something for Him. Instead, you will want to do everything you can to please Him. If you are genuinely in love with Jesus, you will follow and obey Him. It is risky in some cultures to be baptized or baptized again, but the joy and assurance in knowing that He loves you so much for loving Him back in identifying with Him in baptism are worth any suffering.

Questions to consider:

1. Why has water baptism been the source of so much confusion throughout church history?
2. Is baptism important, if at all possible?
3. Can another believe for you and submit to baptism for you, or should one personally do so?
4. Have you ever made a list of all verses in the New Testament on Christian baptism?
5. What did your baptism mean to you when you were baptized? Compare to my list.

CHAPTER 9

SINNING AGAINST
THE HOLY SPIRIT

ॐ

**"But blasphemy against the Holy Spirit
will never be forgiven" (Matt. 12:31).**

B efore going deeper into the work of the Holy Spirit, the seriousness of sinning against the Holy Spirit must be addressed. The scriptures mention several different sins that are frequently committed against the Holy Spirit. Sins against the Holy Spirit are committed as the Holy Spirit operates through our lives or when the Spirit is manifested through the gifts of the Holy Spirit in another's life. In Luke 7:22–23, Jesus is describing His works of healing and deliverance, saying, "And blessed is he who is not offended because of me." We will examine each of these sins against the Holy Spirit individually.

The **first sin** is *resisting the Holy Spirit*. It means to actively oppose, disobey, ignore, or refuse the working or leading of the Holy Spirit. This sin is probably most frequently committed as a personal sin when you resist the operation of the Holy Spirit in your own life. This sin often happens when being drawn or called by the Spirit to surrender your life to Christ, and we resist by putting it off. The Spirit will call again and again, but if we continue in opposing the call to come to Christ, eventually He will no longer draw you to Himself. It also happens when we have been born of the Holy Spirit and sense His leading in following Him in a given direction, and we resist. Sometimes we ignore the leading of the Spirit, and sometimes we may flat-out refuse to obey.

Why do we resist the Holy Spirit? The Bible mentions several reasons. One is *unbelief.*

> Be careful then, dear brothers and sisters. Make sure that your own hearts are not evil and unbelieving, turning you away from the living God. You must warn each other every day, as long as it is still today,' so that none of you will be deceived by sin and hardened against God. (Heb. 3:12, 13; NLT)

After resisting the Spirit for a time, our hearts become hardened. The Bible says three times in a short span, "Today you must listen to his voice. Don't harden your hearts against him" (Heb. 3:7, 8; 3:15; 4:7).

Loving a life of sin over loving life in the light is mentioned in John 3:19: "Their judgment is based on this fact: The light from heaven came into the world, but they loved the darkness more than the light, for their actions were evil."

Human wisdom and thinking is often a reason to resist. It sounds like foolishness compared to worldly wisdom.

> For the message of the cross is foolishness to those who are perishing, but to us who are being saved it is the power of God. For it is written: "I will destroy the wisdom of the wise; the intelligence of

the intelligent I will frustrate." Where is the wise person? Where is the teacher of the law? Where is the philosopher of this age? Has not God made foolish the wisdom of the world? For since in the wisdom of God the world through its wisdom did not know him, God was pleased through the foolishness of what was preached to save those who believe. Jews demand signs and Greeks look for wisdom, but we preach Christ crucified: a stumbling block to Jews and foolishness to Gentiles, but to those whom God has called, both Jews and Greeks, Christ the power of God and the wisdom of God. For the foolishness of God is wiser than human wisdom, and the weakness of God is stronger than human strength. (1Cor. 1:18-25; NIV)

Blinded minds or a veil on the heart are mentioned in 2 Corinthians 3:14, 15, (NKJV), "But their minds were made dull, for to this day, the same veil remains when the old covenant is read. It has not been removed, because only in Christ is it taken away, Even to this day, when Moses is read, a veil covers their hearts."

Second Corinthians 4:3–4 (NKJV) adds to the same thought that the evil one blinds people, causing spiritual blindness: "But even if our gospel is veiled, it is veiled to those who are perishing, whose mind the god of this age has blinded, who do not believe, lest the light of the gospel of the glory of Christ, who is the image of God, should shine on them."

Unfortunately, inadequate teaching and the reduction of Christianity to merely another religion with no personal relationship results in such unawareness.

But what does it say? The word is near you, in your mouth and in your heart (that is, the word of faith which we preach): that if you confess with your mouth the Lord Jesus and believe in your heart that God has raised Him from the dead, you will be saved. For with the heart one believes unto righteousness, and with the mouth confession is made unto salvation. (Rom. 10:8–10; NKJV)

Without adequate teaching, people will resist the drawing of the Holy Spirit because they never heard the way of salvation. Jesus also warns to beware of the education of religious leaders. We need to read the Bible for ourselves, making sure we are fully receiving the truth.

Resisting the Holy Spirit can have serious consequences. Consider the story of Stephen in Acts 6 and 7. Stephen was a man full of the Holy Spirit and wisdom with great faith. Religious people tried to debate with him concerning his faith, but no one could stand against his wisdom and Spirit by which he spoke. As lies were being brought against him, he was brought before the religious high council, and his face became as bright as an angel's. After a lengthy address of the nation's history, he replied, "You stiff-necked people, with uncircumcised hearts and ears! You are just like your fathers: You always resist the Holy Spirit!" (Acts 7:51; NIV).

His reply sounds very harsh and politically incorrect. But remember, he made his statements filled with the Holy Spirit while God the Holy Spirit caused his face to shine with His glory. Remember also that these strong words of Stephen were spoken after the crowd saw Stephen perform amazing miracles and signs by the power of the Holy Spirit. The sin of resistance is extremely dangerous when committed while powerful manifestations of the

Holy Spirit are displayed. The fullness of such sin is to blaspheme the Holy Spirit, the unforgivable sin, which we will consider last.

The **second sin** against the Holy Spirit is *grieving the Holy Spirit.* This sin means to bring sorrow or distress to the Holy Spirit. "And do not grieve the Holy Spirit of God, with whom you were sealed for the day of redemption" (Eph. 4:30; NIV). The statement is a command in the original language. It breaks God's heart because He desires intimacy, and the Holy Spirit provides such intimacy with God. The next verse, 30, explains some actions that grieve the Holy Spirit within us: "Get rid of all bitterness, rage, and anger, brawling and slander, along with every form of malice," and verse 32 says, "Be kind and compassionate to one another, forgiving each other, just as in Christ God forgave you."

If we are in love with God and Jesus, we will not take the gift of the Holy Spirit lightly. We will live for Him and "throw off the old evil nature, our former way of life, which is rotten through and through, full of lust and deception" (Eph. 4:22; NLT). Reading Ephesians 4:17–32 gives an excellent incentive to eliminate this sin in our lives.

A **third sin** against the Holy Spirit is *quenching the Holy Spirit.* It means to extinguish or to put out the fire of the Holy Spirit. Quenching is the same word as used in Matthew 25 when speaking of the five virgin's lamps going out. We certainly can put out the fire in our lives by ignoring the Spirit's fire until the light goes out, or a person can ignore the calling of the Spirit on their life. One can ignore the charismatic gift, the gifts within them as listed in 1 Corinthians 12. If we do not stir up the gift within us, the fire goes out.

However, most frequently, I see this sin committed against other believers. I have heard things about new, excited believers like, "Give them a little time, and they will cool off," which is pretty passive but indicates disapproval of the fire in the life of another. There are much more aggressive actions also. There exists criticism that shows dissatisfaction of exuberance in worship styles, such as raising hands, bowing down, clapping, and so forth. There exists harsh criticism in the church at times of the manifestation of the gifts of the Holy Spirit. We may notice strong disapproval, saying that the gifts of the Holy Spirit have ceased since the completion of the writing of scripture. Theologically, this teaching is called cessation. The Bible says, "Do not put out the Spirit's fire; do not treat prophecy with contempt" (1 Thess. 5:19, 20; NIV). One should never quench the working of the Spirit personally or in another's life.

Any of the three sins against the Holy Spirit mentioned above are dangerous. We will now look at the **fourth sin** against the Spirit, *blasphemy of the Holy Spirit*. This sin is most dangerous because it is called an unforgivable sin in scripture. The other three can potentially lead to the desecration of the Holy Spirit. The Holy Spirit is God's unique gift to believers and precious to God the Father. There have been various explanations offered on what the sin of blasphemy against the Holy Spirit is. I treat this with extreme caution because of the severity of this sin. There is no other sin as grave as an unforgivable sin.

There are only three instances in scripture, indicating forgiveness is not granted. Everyone is aware that eternity will be spent in hell if one does not receive Christ. Therefore, many claim this to be the unpardonable sin. Indeed, there is no forgiveness if salvation is not received in faith, but it is not blasphemy of the Holy Spirit. The Bible also says that if one takes the mark of the beast, they will be unforgiven (Rev. 14:9–13); this is not blasphemy of the Holy Spirit either.

Blasphemy means to dishonor, slander, or irreverence the Holy Spirit with a critical, defiant attitude through words or actions. We need to be on the alert for this sin, especially with the manifestation of the gifts, or if deliverance takes place. That is what happened when Jesus warned of the seriousness of this sin. We must consider the context of the words of Jesus. When people say that the gifts of the Spirit or any working of the Spirit are from Satan, that person is on very slippery ground. That is what the Pharisees did when Jesus called out the sin of blasphemy against the Holy Spirit. It is necessary to understand what blasphemy of the Holy Spirit is in the context of scripture and how it is used.

Jesus was casting out demons when the religious leaders declared that Jesus did it by the power of Satan. Jesus went on to explain the impossibility of their thinking. Then, He goes on to say, "Every sin or blasphemy can be forgiven—except blasphemy against the Holy Spirit, which can never be forgiven. Anyone who blasphemes against me, the Son of Man, can be forgiven, but blasphemy against the Holy Spirit will never be forgiven, either in this world or in the world to come" (Matt. 12:31, 32; NLT).

Be very cautious about what you say concerning the baptism of the Holy Spirit, speaking in tongues, prophecy, healings, deliverance, or any other gift of the Spirit. Be careful what you say about praise and worship music or the old hymns, many of which were inspired by the Holy Spirit while the author was in the presence of God.

Remember, the Holy Spirit is very special to God the Father in that blasphemy of his Son can be forgiven, but blasphemy against the Holy Spirit cannot be forgiven. That is amazing and thought-provoking to think blasphemy against Jesus can be forgiven but not against the Holy Spirit. When someone observes the work of the Holy Spirit, it should never be said that it is the work of Satan.

Giving Satan credit for the work of the Holy Spirit is a dangerous path, quickly leading to a hardened heart. My personal feeling is that anyone sorry that he has offended the Holy Spirit of God does not have a hard-enough heart to have committed this sin, and I pray that I am not too soft on this point, but I desire to extend grace for He is full of grace and truth. Do not cross the line or even get close to it. I feel it is necessary to share about sinning against the Holy Spirit before going into the work of the Holy Spirit in my life and the scriptures so that no one will unknowingly put down the work of the Holy Spirit.

Questions to consider:

1. Did you know that you can sin against the Holy Spirit as well as God?
2. Which of the four sins against the Holy Spirit are you most likely to commit?
3. Have you ever been concerned that you have committed the unpardonable sin? You would not be reading this if you think you had committed it.
4. Have you ever warned others to be very careful about sinning against the Holy Spirit, or has anyone ever warned you?
5. How has this chapter helped you?

CHAPTER 10

HOLY SPIRIT BAPTISM

"Jesus said, 'John baptized with water, but in a few days you will be baptized in the Holy Spirit'" (Acts 1:5; NIV).

This topic is very dear to the heart of God and my heart as well. The baptism in the Holy Spirit has revolutionized my life as it has many believers. More importantly, this is God's extravagant gift to all who have been born of the Holy Spirit. This gift enables us to be lavish in returning love to God and others. To an unbeliever, the greatest gift is the gift of eternal life. Once the gift of eternal life is received, the greatest gift to believers is the gift of the Holy Spirit.

The Bible states that power is received when you receive the gift of the Holy Spirit—power in word and deed to love God and others. It is a gift enabling a greater intimacy with the Father and the Son and the Holy Spirit, a holy romance! First love is the first concern in the first letter to the first church addressed in the book of Revelation. It is also the first and greatest commandment and is to be kept in first place. God's greatest desire is to have intimacy with His children, and He provides the way through the gift of the Holy Spirit.

Immediately after being born of the Holy Spirit, I experienced an overpowering hunger for the Word of God. Being born of the Holy Spirit was my primary interest. There were two other topics the Spirit strongly emphasized as significant. First was the Holy Spirit, and the second was the second coming of Jesus. I knew nothing about either one, but the Spirit highlighted these topics. There were many other topics of interest as well, but these two stood out.

Having never heard any teaching on these topics, I began to study and dig through the scripture on my own. I noticed the Holy Spirit and the second coming were big deals to God. Both produced much excitement as I studied. The Holy Spirit generated excitement because it gave power and exhilaration in this life on earth. The second coming was exciting because I could not wait to meet Jesus who saved me, and I desired to see Him face-to-face and to spend eternity with Him.

The powers of darkness, which are led by the father of lies, had produced in the church, and in myself, many false concepts about this most precious gift of the Holy Spirit. The devil and the powers of darkness greatly fear believers receiving this gift. It is the power that defeats evil forces. After John the Baptist baptized Jesus, the Holy Spirit descended like a dove and alighted upon Jesus (Matthew 3:16). His ministry began undoing the works of the devil. "After the baptism that John preached—how God anointed Jesus of Nazareth with the Holy Spirit and power, and how he went around doing good and healing all who were under the power of the devil, because God was with him" (Acts 10:37,38).

As church history progressed, it appeared to the many leaders and theologians of the church that the gifts of the Spirit were no longer active. Rather than examining the scriptures and going through self-examination of their state of spirituality, they made teachings that fit their experience. They proclaimed that the gifts of the Holy Spirit had ceased after the writing of scripture. This teaching or doctrine is called *cessation,* which means the gifts have ceased to operate. This teaching was readily accepted and is still widely accepted globally to this day.

Along with cessation, it seemed consistent to declare the baptism in the Holy Spirit is no longer a viable gift or that it is now automatic when one becomes a believer. Strangely, part of the working of the Holy Spirit was still in operation, and the section on the teaching of the baptism in the Spirit and the gifts as listed in 1 Corinthians 12 were declared not operative. The instigation of such teaching is very smart on the part of the evil one, which results in believers being powerless to undo the works of Satan. Satan has no problem with powerless believers, enabling the devil greater freedom to carry out his evil schemes on earth. But Jesus came to defeat the powers of darkness and commanded us to continue His ministry, which is the reason and purpose for the gifts of the Holy Spirit. Other teachings also arose and were incorporated into the church because they seemed reasonable and relevant for that time, not because it was taught in scripture.

There also arose teaching that the book of Acts is not for doctrine; only the Epistles are useful for doctrine and teaching. But, the Bible says that all Scripture is God-breathed, meaningful, and useful for doctrine and teaching (2 Tim. 3:16). The book of Acts is the foundation for the Epistles. It all begins with the book of Acts. For example, the beginning of the Corinthians is in chapter 18 of Acts. The origin of Ephesians is in Acts 19. All the teachings in the Epistles are based on what is taught in the book of Acts. The Acts of the Apostles is crucial in understanding scripture accurately. It is God's blueprint for the church.

There were many objections to the baptism in the Holy Spirit in the 1970s when I was wrestling with the concept. Some called it the second blessing, while others said that was impossible because salvation is the only blessing. Frankly, I have been blessed hundreds of times, not just once. God's blessings are never-ending; they are new every morning. Others objected to the word *baptism* and preferred the word *filled*. There was confusion between the baptism in the Holy Spirit and water baptism, thinking they were the same or occurred at the same time. That thought existed in both camps of infant baptism and believer's water baptism.

The wording *one baptism* in Ephesians 4:5 has many confused. I repeat, we need to take all of the scripture on this point of the "one baptism" to get an accurate understanding. We must consider other scripture that speaks to this issue. First Corinthians 12:13 clearly states, "For we are all baptized by one Spirit into one body." The baptism into the body by the Spirit happens when we are born of God and is the "one baptism." "There is one body and one Spirit, just as you were called to one hope when you were called; one Lord, one faith, one baptism; one God and Father of all, who is over all and through all and in all" (Eph. 4:4–5; NIV).

It happens at the time of salvation, "when you are called," and you respond in faith; that is the one baptism into the one body. It is a matter of reading accurately and not a matter of interpretation. "For by one Spirit, we were all baptized into one body, whether Jews or Greeks, whether slaves or free, and we were all made to drink of the one Spirit" (1 Cor. 12:13; NASB).

Consider Hebrews 6:2 NKJV, and notice the plural form of the word *baptism*; "the doctrine of baptisms." This passage speaks of more than one baptism. What does that mean? In looking up the word *baptism* in all of the scripture, we observe more than one baptism. Pay careful attention to the prepositions, what a person is baptized into, and by whom. We are baptized into the "one body by the one Spirit" (which is by the Holy Spirit when we are born of the Holy Spirit). We are baptized in water by another believer, and we are baptized in the Holy Spirit by Jesus. As you search scripture on the word *baptism*, you will also notice the baptism of suffering, persecution, the least popular of all the baptisms. But, the "one baptism" is into the one body of Christ by the one Spirit when we are born from above and does not mean water baptism or Spirit baptism. To be baptized into the body means to be immersed into Christ's body. Nor does "one baptism," mean all the baptisms are lumped into one baptism.

The apostles battled against teachings based on human tradition, philosophy, and worldly principals at the time of the writing of scripture. After centuries of teachings by men, such error would only increase and be magnified. Therefore it is necessary to return to scripture regardless of our human thinking. The Bible says, "See to it that no one takes you captive through hollow and deceptive philosophy which depends on human tradition and the basic principles of this world rather than on Christ" (Col. 2:8; NIV).

Let us look at what the Bible has to say about the continuing of the gifts of the Spirit. The Bible states that the gifts of the Holy Spirit will continue until the second coming of Christ. They will not cease when the disciples die but will continue until Jesus returns. "Therefore you do not lack any spiritual gift as you eagerly wait for our Lord Jesus Christ to be revealed" (1 Cor. 1:7; NIV).

Also, in 1 Corinthians 12:10 (NLT), we read, "But when the end comes, these special gifts will all disappear." These passages clearly show that the gifts will continue until Christ returns. The early church needed the gifts of the Spirit, and the church today needs them just as much or more. The power of the Spirit will indeed be necessary immediately before the return of Christ. The later outpouring of the Holy Spirit prophesied in scripture will also be the cause of great persecution. We need special preparation for the days ahead, and the gifts of the Spirit will be essential for our perseverance. Human effort will be to no avail. Read Matthew

THE ENTRANCE INTO THE KINGDOM

24:9–11 to gain knowledge of the incredible persecution that will take place before Jesus returns, greater than anything that has ever taken place before this time. The bride of Christ will be armed and ready only through the power of the Holy Spirit.

The baptism of the Holy Spirit should not be confused with the new birth. Being born again is a work of the Holy Spirit and is also called "born of the Spirit," but it is not the baptism of the Holy Spirit. The word *baptism* means to be "completely immersed." It means to be saturated, not merely a sprinkling or pouring. Baptism has the same meaning as placing a cloth in a dye solution. You immerse the fabric into the dye until the dye has wholly saturated every fiber of the material. Then it is removed out of the solution. To be soaked by the Spirit is the picture of the baptism in the Holy Spirit. It means wholly immersed in the Spirit of God as the Spirit comes upon us. There are no modes, as some teach, to the word *baptism*; it means drenched or saturated.

The promised Holy Spirit needs to be received, and it is a gift which must be accepted in faith just like the gift of salvation "so that by faith we might receive the promise of the Spirit" (Gal. 3:14). Also, notice in the book of Acts that when people believed and were baptized, Peter and John came to lay hands on those who had already believed so they could receive the Holy Spirit. Notice the baptism of the Holy Spirit is always after one believes and a gift which is separate from being born of the Holy Spirit, which must occur first. When a person receives Christ, the Holy Spirit enters the human spirit, and you are born again or born of the Holy Spirit. But upon examining all accounts in scripture, we observe that the baptism of the Holy Spirit comes after the new birth. Therefore, the baptism in the Holy Spirit is not the entrance of the Spirit when receiving Christ, but a later emersion.

The basis for believing that it is all one experience comes from Acts 2:38, which reads in the NKJV, "Repent, and let every one of you be baptized in the name of Jesus Christ for the remission of sins; and you shall receive the gift of the Holy Spirit." Some translations use the word *will* in place of *shall*, making it more difficult to understand. In studying commentaries by men with a variety of Ph.D. degrees and in particular, the original languages, agree that the word *shall* is a command, as in the Ten Commandments that state, you shall have no other Gods before me. It means, "and, you shall then take the step of receiving the gift of the Holy Spirit."

The translation as a command is consistent with the practice by the disciples in the book of Acts. The interpretation that the baptism in the Holy Spirit is automatic at the time of the new birth is not compatible with the practice of sending for Peter and John to come and lay hands on those who had believed. Notice in all incidents, believing and water baptism quickly led to receiving the gift of the Holy Spirit as soon as it was understood. It was a part of the proper initiation into the kingdom. What an awesome God, giving such good gifts to humanity! The gift is for as many as the Lord our God will call. If you are one of His called, it is for you!

Also, consider the question in Acts 19:2; Paul asked some disciples, "Did you receive the Holy Spirit when you believed?" The question would not exist if the baptism of the Holy Spirit were automatically received when receiving the gift of eternal life. The Bible says in Acts 19:5–6, "It was then explained to them, and they were baptized again in the name of the Lord Jesus. After that, Paul placed his hands on them, and the Holy Spirit came on them, and they spoke in other tongues and prophesied."

In Acts 8, there is a longer gap between believing and receiving the Spirit. Verses 12–16 explain that the Samaritans believed, and they were baptized. When the apostles in Jerusalem heard that Samaria had received the Word of God, they sent Peter and John to them. When they arrived, they prayed for them that they might receive the Holy Spirit because the Holy Spirit had not yet come upon them. So they placed their hands on them, and they received the Holy Spirit. It was not received at the time of believing and responding in water baptism.

The baptism of the Holy Spirit is mentioned by John the Baptist in all four gospels, calling attention to the significance of this gift. John the Baptist said that he baptized in water, but after him would come someone who baptizes in the Holy Spirit. At Jesus's water baptism, as He was coming up out of the water, the Holy Spirit descended upon Him. The Father approved this sequence by the voice coming from heaven, saying, "You are my Son, whom I love: with you, I am well pleased" (Luke 1:11). Jesus set the example and pattern for us.

Jesus prophesied in John 7:38–39 (NIV):

> On the last and greatest day of the feast, Jesus stood and said in a loud voice, "If anyone is thirsty, let him come to me and drink. Whoever believes in me as the scripture has said, streams of living water will flow from within him." By this, He meant the Spirit, whom those who believed in Him were later to receive. Up to that time, the Spirit had not been given since Jesus had not yet been glorified.

Are you thirsty? Do you desire the rivers of living water, the Holy Spirit to flow from your innermost being? Receive this gift by permitting Jesus to baptize you!

Just before Jesus ascended to heaven, He gave the disciples specific instructions and information concerning the promised Holy Spirit. Think of the significance of His final preparations before leaving this earth. Indeed my last direction, given the opportunity, would be what is most concerning to me. These were the final instructions and, therefore, most important to Jesus as He was going to ascend to the right hand of the Father. In teaching Jesus made statements about the Spirit that are profound like:

> I tell you the truth, anyone who believes in me will do the same works I have done. He will do even greater things than these because I am going to the Father. You can ask for anything in my name, and I will do it, so that the Son can bring glory to the Father. You may ask anything in my name, and I will do it, so that the Son can bring glory to the Father, Yes, ask me for anything in my name, and I will do it! (John 14:12–14; NLT)

Read John, chapters 14–17, for Jesus's final instructions and prayer for all who will believe. In context, His teaching is for entirely devoted followers of Jesus, not merely for any and everybody as it were a vending machine.

Jesus also speaks about the promised gift of the Holy Spirit immediately before ascending to heaven, again emphasizing the importance of the gift:

> Jesus said, "Do not leave Jerusalem but wait for the gift my Father promised, which you have heard me speak about. For John baptized with water, but in a few days, you will be baptized with the Holy Spirit. … But you will receive power when the Holy Spirit comes on you, and you will be my witnesses in Jerusalem, and in all Judea and Samaria, to the ends of the earth." (Acts 1:4–5, 8; NIV)

The gift is a gift of power to proclaim the gospel to the ends of the earth. Jesus's final commands were to go and witness. First, wait for the promised Holy Spirit and then go to testify in the power of Jesus's Spirit. They followed the instruction given by Jesus with the results recorded in the book of Acts.

> The apostles performed many miraculous signs and wonders among the people. (Acts 5:12; NIV)

> As a result, people brought the sick into the streets and laid them on beds and mats so that at least Peter's shadow might fall on some of them as he passed by. (Acts 5:15; NIV)

> Crowds also gathered from the towns around Jerusalem, bringing their sick and those tormented by evil spirits, and all of them were healed. (Acts 5:15–16; NIV)

That was the power to witness of which Jesus spoke, and the results were phenomenal. In addition to the twelve, we see others following the commands of Jesus using the power of the Holy Spirit. "So Paul and Barnabas spent considerable time there, speaking boldly for the Lord, who confirmed the message of His grace by enabling them to do miraculous signs and wonders" (Acts 14:3; NIV).

We have lost sight of witnessing in the power of the Holy Spirit through centuries of inadequate teachings in the church. We need to repent and return to the Word of God to fulfill the Great Commission in this day of lawlessness.

In the early 1970s, as I continued to search the scriptures and communicate with others in Bible study groups, I came across a book in our church library entitled *Like A Mighty Wind* by Mel Tari. That was the first book I read about the Holy Spirit, and it was

just like the stories I read in the Bible! It was about miracles, healings, deliverance, signs, and wonders in the Indonesian revival!
After that, I found a few more books in bookstores on the Holy
Spirit. Testimonies are powerful, defeating the works of Satan
(Rev. 12:11). Later, I learned that these books were written as the
charismatic movement kicked in gear. The Jesus movement was
also in full swing. What a beautiful, exciting time to be living. I
continued to study until I was thoroughly convinced that the gift
of the Holy Spirit was good for today and was God's love gift and
His intense desire for all believers.

Understand how I was raised—accepting the truth in the scriptures on receiving the Holy Spirit "as they did in the beginning"
was an unthinkable step. It was contrary to the teaching I had
received, even looked down upon, and considered a strange doctrine. But I was fully convicted and convinced from the Word of
God to receive this precious gift: the promised Holy Spirit "for all
who are far off and called by the Lord our God" (Acts 2:39). I was
not yet on board with the speaking in tongues as a manifestation
of the gift. However, I was not only ready but excited to receive
God's love and joy in the gift of the Holy Spirit.

My Testimony in Receiving the Baptism in the Holy Spirit

One night when I got home from Bible study, I was fully
expecting to receive the gift of the Holy Spirit and very excited
to ask. I was fully convinced and knew Jesus would baptize me!
I laid flat on my back, looking up as I began to pray. With great
excitement, I told God that I was ready to receive His mighty baptism in the Spirit. I requested, "Jesus, do something extraordinary
so that I know without a doubt that You baptized me in the Holy
Spirit." I also told Him, "I did not want to speak in tongues but

rather to bestow on me the gift of healing, which seemed to be much more practical." I'm sure God, knowing my heart, smiled, and in His extravagant love for me said, "Okay, my son, I will do as you have requested, but I will show you the more excellent way."

Even after telling God how to do it, in His great love, He granted my request because He knew I was, in a sense, a pioneer and had not had any Holy Spirit teaching to "explain the way of God more adequately" (Acts 18:26). As I lay on my back with hands raised and said, "Okay, Jesus, baptize me in the Holy Spirit." Suddenly there was a roar, increasing in volume, like a train approaching and going right by me, and then the sound gradually decreased. At the same time, I experienced a bright light shining on me. I had my eyes closed, but you know how it is when a bright light is shining directly on your closed eyes. You can sense the light shining through your eyelids, which is the way I experienced it. Simultaneously, a jolt went through my chest, and later I realized that healing of my bronchitis took place! I was having a severe case of bronchitis at the time, which I often had but have never had again after that night.

What an incredible confirmation! God is so good and faithful! He did abundantly more than I asked or could even imagine Him doing. I would never have thought of asking for everything He did and accomplished at that moment. And, I didn't speak in tongues. The Holy Spirit is like a perfect gentleman and did not do more than I was willing to receive. (All you hardcore Pentecostals, hang in there. You will need to read the chapter on "Praying in the Spirit" to get the rest of the story.) Do not expect God to do the same thing and in the same way each time He baptizes someone in the Holy Spirit. God has enough resources to accomplish a unique experience for each person, as He sees fit and necessary.

Hearing others share their testimony in receiving the baptism in the Spirit, I realized my experience was unique. The reasons may be multiple. The Lord saw what I needed. The age in which I lived with much opposition, maybe for centuries, might be a likely reason. There was also a lack of teaching at that time, which ended up being a plus since I had to dig everything out from scripture for myself. He may have desired me to dig it out of scripture rather than receiving information secondhand. I also think that perhaps God was looking into the future and has a particular assignment that may require such a powerful and unique experience. I can only speculate, but it is not because I deserved something special, but because of His grace and plan, and I will have to wait to know fully. Our knowledge is incomplete even with the gifts of the Spirit until the day we understand fully (1 Cor. 13:12).

Being born of the Spirit was already an incredible experience. I was so in love with Jesus and wanted to know everything about Him and to do whatever I could do to know and please Him more. My first love for Him was so intense, so how could the baptism in the Holy Spirit benefit me more than this? The blessings of the baptism in the Holy Spirit are many.

The Word of God was so exciting preceding my baptism in the Spirit; one may wonder how it could increase? I experienced an extra degree of sensitivity to the study and reading of the Word following the baptism. The Word of God was so alive and convincing. Often the Spirit would move me to tears as I read God's Word. I would experience extreme conviction and comfort. Everything in His Word was so encouraging and uplifting. I was becoming acquainted intimately with Him through revelations by the Holy Spirit.

There was also a supernatural revelation taking place; God was speaking to me personally. I heard the voice of God much more. The still, small voice was just as loud as the audible voice. Which voice it was made no difference; it was real. The Word became very personal between the Lord and me. Many times He would also talk to me when working or whatever I was doing. He would give words of wisdom, knowledge, and discernment. When I say the Spirit spoke to me, I do not mean some sort of a hunch or some natural form of knowledge, but a supernatural revelation. It may take some experience and time to identify the difference. But, there comes a time when you will discern and know the voice of the Lord.

The baptism in the Spirit helped me to be continually tuned in to the right frequency enabling me to hear Him speak at any time. It would happen during regular activities outside of reading scripture and prayer time. God would often speak prophetically to me even before I fully understood prophecy. When Jesus baptized me in the Holy Spirit, remember, I told God I didn't want to speak in tongues without realizing that not only is tongues a manifestation of the baptism, but so is prophecy (Acts 19:6). I experienced prophecy concerning the future often, and it would come true in detail.

One evening as I was reading scripture, the Spirit broke in and spoke a word that stunned me. The Spirit said, "In thirty days, your pastor would be exposed for secret sin in his life." I loved my pastor, who preached powerful, convicting sermons. It was under this pastor's ministry that I came to the Lord. Frankly, I did not want this to be the voice of the Spirit. It was very unsettling. So, I wrote it down and dated it, thinking I've got to see it to believe it. On the thirtieth day, three women individually called me on the same day, sharing about their immoral involvement with our pastor.

I was a deacon in our church at the time and not an ordained elder. I was curious as to why they would call me and not one of the elders. God was working in me to convince me that He was all-knowing and would reveal the truth to anyone with an ear to hear what the Spirit was saying. The Bible says, "Do not scoff at prophecies, but test everything that is said. Hold on to what is good" (1Thess. 5:21; NLT).

Frequently, the Holy Spirit speaks in surprising ways. He will enlighten you in understanding what you did not understand earlier. He will call out things you particularly do not want to hear. The Spirit will inform you of things that will happen in the future for which you had no idea. He will speak fresh revelations to you. The Holy Spirit will never speak anything contrary to scripture.

The baptism in the Holy Spirit gives supernatural power in your personal life to overcome sin. It helps to identify sins that you may have excused in the past or did not even consider something to be a sin. Conviction, which is a function of the Holy Spirit, is sharpened as the Lord speaks to you.

The baptism in the Holy Spirit produced a desire in me to be reconciled in relationships with anyone I wronged. I wanted to be restored and felt the need to apologize to those I had hurt. I asked the Holy Spirit to bring to my remembrance all who I had wronged. I got rapid answers on that request. Whoever the Spirit brought to my attention, I approached and confessed. Confession brought genuine peace in my life. It was a burden to carry the sin, knowing you had wronged someone and had not asked forgiveness.

The baptism in the Holy Spirit not only enhances the supernatural gifts of the Holy Spirit as recorded in First Corinthians 12, 13, and 14, but also provides more significant growth in the fruit of the Spirit. One cannot have the fruit of the Spirit without the Spirit. Many have said that one needs to work at producing the fruit of the Spirit. Does an apple tree have to work at producing apples, or will it create something else, like peaches? No, it just produces apples because that is what an apple tree does. It's natural for it to produce apples.

It is the same way for each of us. When the Spirit is within, we naturally produce the fruit of the Spirit because that is our new nature. It is also helpful to remember that the fruit of the Spirit is as supernatural as the gifts. The love within you as a believer should be different from the natural love you had as a non-regenerate person. The fruit is undoubtedly evident after experiencing the new birth; however, my observation was that following the baptism in the Holy Spirit, the fruit was enhanced and more natural rather than something I produced by trying harder.

In the natural, it is easy to favor the fruit over the gifts, enabling us to justify our shortcomings. When it comes to gifts and fruit, people like to emphasize one or the other and say the fruit is more important or the gifts are more important. The Bible offers no favoritism of one over the other. The will of God the Spirit is for both; they go together. The work of the Spirit desires to accomplish both. It is not one over the other but both.

Notice also that the fruit of the Spirit is singular, not plural (Gal. 5:22–23). That means it is one, a package deal. You get them all. We may, in our humanness, have allowed one to exceed another, which is not the way it should be. We need to permit the Spirit to produce all of the fruit in our lives. The gifts of the Spirit are plural, and the Spirit manifests each as He wills for the common good. "All of these are the work of the same Spirit, and He gives them to each one, as He determines" (1 Cor. 12:11).

In reading scripture, each of the apostles manifested all of the gifts but not at the same time. According to 1 Corinthians 14, in an individual church service where time is limited, one person will come with one gift, the next person with another gift, and those who speak in tongues or prophesy may do so one at a time and only two or at most three in one meeting.

The baptism in the Holy Spirit is the source of power in the believer. The power is to witness in word and deed. When sharing Jesus with someone after receiving the baptism in the Holy Spirit, I noticed my words had a more significant impact on both believers and unbelievers. We are empowered to witness (Acts 1:8). The powers of darkness are not effective when confronted by the testimony of believers full of the Holy Spirit (Rev. 12:11). The Spirit gives wisdom and just the right words, often prophetic words and specific revelation.

As we get into the book of Acts, we see that the apostles had the power of Jesus to do the works that He did. It didn't stop with the apostles but continued with Stephen, Philip, and Paul with his missionary teams. Signs and wonders followed their teachings about Jesus, confirming their words. "The reason the Son of God appeared was to destroy the works of the devil" (1John 3:8; NLT).

Most important of all, the baptism in the Holy Spirit enhances your relationship with the Lord. His greatest desire for us is to be in a deep love relationship with Him. That is why He created us. Can you think of a more exciting relationship than intimately knowing the creator of the universe, the King of kings, and Lord of lords? Why would you not desire the baptism in the Holy Spirit? Jesus voluntarily took the curse for us and was hung on the cross so that we can have the promised Holy Spirit and be an overcomer. Jesus paid a high price for the promised Holy Spirit, knowing it's a necessity to defeat evil and carry on the ministry of Jesus in our hurting world.

Questions to consider:

1. Why is the baptism in the Holy Spirit so important to Jesus? See 1 John 3:8 and Acts 1:8. Name two things mentioned here.
2. So why does Satan hate the power of the Holy Spirit so much?
3. What does Satan want us to believe concerning the baptism in the Holy Spirit?

4. What kind of false teachings rose against the baptism in the Holy Spirit over the history of the church? Why?

5. Why is it so important to examine all of scripture concerning the Holy Spirit?

6. How long will the gifts of the Holy Spirit continue? See 1 Corinthians 1:7; 12:10

7. Have you considered the baptism in the Holy Spirit is for greater intimacy with God?

8. Why was Jesus willing to pay such a great price by hanging on the Cross for us to acquire the promised Holy Spirit (the baptism in the Holy Spirit)? See Galatians 3:13, 14.

CHAPTER 11

RECEIVING THE BAPTISM IN
THE HOLY SPIRIT

కింగ

**"How much more will your Father in heaven give the Holy
Spirit to those who ask Him" (Luke 11:13 NIV).**

Receiving the baptism in the Holy Spirit is the Father's greatest
desire for all who have accepted Jesus into their heart. John
the Baptist made a big deal of Jesus coming to baptize in the Holy
Spirit. There are also many places in the Old Testament, predicting
the outpouring of the Holy Spirit. Jesus also made a big deal of
the Holy Spirit in His teaching and by His example of receiving
the Holy Spirit. The Holy Spirit came upon Him when John the
Baptist baptized Him in water. In His teaching, Jesus talked about
the Holy Spirit, especially immediately before His crucifixion and
in His last words before leaving this earth to return to the Father.

Jesus instructed His disciples on the Holy Spirit a lot during
His earthly ministry. He taught about essential concepts, like the
seriousness of blaspheming the Holy Spirit and the role of the Holy
Spirit in the ministry of healing and in casting out demons. Right
before Jesus went to the cross, He taught them on the coming of

the Holy Spirit. It was the last thing Jesus said immediately before leaving and ascending to heaven. Jesus only said what He heard the Father saying; therefore, these are words from the Father also. Jesus taught about the Holy Spirit because the Holy Spirit enables a deep intimacy with the Father.

Jesus ascended to the Father so that we could have this incredible gift. The twelve disciples watched Jesus minister for about three and a half years. How exciting would such an opportunity be? Could there be anything more significant? Yes, according to Jesus, the coming of the Holy Spirit at Pentecost. "Jesus said, 'Nevertheless I tell you the truth. It is to your advantage that I go away; for if I do not go away, the Helper (the Holy Spirit) will not come to you; but if I depart, I will send Him to you'" (John 16:7; NKJV).

Jesus had to return to the Father to receive the Holy Spirit from the Father so that He could baptize us in the Holy Spirit. The Father and the Son are very intentional about sending the Holy Spirit. It is His will to equip us to continue the ministry Jesus started. Acts 2:38 (NKJV) says, "You shall receive the gift of the Holy Spirit." In the original language, that statement is a command, not an automatic occurrence.

It is a good thing if you desire the baptism in the Holy Spirit. There are several things you should do before receiving it. You must be sure your heart is ready and clean to avoid confusion. The first is very obvious. Make sure that you have been born again and that Jesus is the Lord of your life. The baptism in the Holy Spirit is for believers only. It is essential to repent, confess your sins, and to invite Jesus into your heart, giving Him full control of your life. If Jesus is not Lord of all, He is not Lord at all. If there are unbelief and uncertainty about your salvation, the result may be much confusion between conflicting spirits and even turmoil in your life. A fully surrendered heart is the Lord's desire for the gift of eternal life and the gift of the Holy Spirit.

Second, make sure there is no unconfessed sin in your life. Confession of all sin is important; getting it in the open, exposing it to the light; otherwise, the devil will have ground to attack you with doubts and lies. From experience and the Word of God, there is something called the old nature that conflicts with the new nature. The battle is real. Do not walk in the flesh, but walk in the Spirit. If you have wronged anyone, ask for forgiveness and make restitution where necessary. If you have been wronged or abused by anyone, you need to forgive and receive inner healing. The last thing you want is a different spirit manifesting itself. Do not give the devil a foothold into your life. (Read Matt. 5:24; 6:22–26; Mark 11:22–26; Acts 5:32.)

Third, make sure you renounce all demonic activities in your past and present life. Americans are especially unaware of the spirit world and the war in the heavenly realms. These practices will shock some people; however, they are strictly forbidden in Deuteronomy 18. Fortune telling by any means, horoscopes, the Ouija board, table lifting, Spiritism, out of body experiences, New Age practices and books, Dungeons and Dragons (and similar games), hypnosis, blood pacts or cutting yourself intentionally, martial arts, Yoga, black or white magic, superstitions, and false religions, must all be renounced in Jesus's name. This list is only partial, but you get the idea. God is a jealous God when it comes to the worship of any other god. All other gods are strictly forbidden. Check out some of these scripture verses: Deuteronomy 18:10–14; Acts 19:13–20; Isaiah 61:1; Matthew 12:45; Matthew 23:31, 36; and Mark 3:27.

Ask the Holy Spirit to bring to mind any offenses you may have committed. Pray a prayer of repentance for each of these involvements that the Holy Spirit brings to your mind. Pray out loud along these lines, filling in the blanks with everything the Spirit brings to your mind, and for each offense:

> Lord I confess that I have been involved with
> _____. I know it was evil and offensive in your sight. I ask for your forgiveness. In the name of the Lord Jesus, I renounce my relationship with _____. I cancel out all ground that the enemy has gained in my life through this involvement. I thank you for forgiving me. In Jesus's name, amen.

For example, Lord, I confess that I have been involved with *the Ouija board.* I know this is evil and offensive in your sight. I ask for your forgiveness. In the name of the Lord Jesus, I renounce my relationship with *the Ouija board.* I cancel out all ground that the enemy has gained in my life through this involvement. I thank you for forgiving me, in Jesus's name, amen. Renouncing such practices may be a new level of repentance for you. But, do this whether you are receiving the Holy Spirit or not. If you never prayed such prayers, they will set you free.

Fourth, get rid of all addictions. These are strongholds in your life. Seek deliverance with the assistance of reliable and trusted people. Anything that ranks above God in your life is a stronghold that needs to go. We usually think of drugs and alcohol as the only addictions, but there are many more, including things like sports. And yes, pornography is a massive issue in this day with all our technology. When over fifty percent of pastors regularly view porn, we have a severe problem. This addiction is no less powerful than drugs. These bondages are powerful forces, and action must be taken to eliminate them from your life. Get rid of all evil materials. Clean up your computers and phones. Pray prayers of deliverance as with other demonic activities in the third step. Ask the Holy Spirit to bring to your remembrance all strongholds in your life.

> Many who became believers confessed their sinful practices. A number of them who had been practicing sorcery brought their incantation books and burned them at a public bonfire. The value of the books was several million dollars. So the message about the Lord spread widely and had a powerful effect. (Acts 19:18–20; NLT)

Fifth, make sure that you renounce all evil passed down to you from your forefathers. Exodus 20:5 tells us that God visits the sins of the forefathers down to the third and fourth generation. You may not be aware of specific ancestral sins. So pray a simple prayer like this: "In the name of the Lord Jesus, I renounce all demonic relationships, evil practices, and sins that have come down from my ancestors and cancel out all ground that the enemy has gained in my life through such generational sins."

Repentance is critical. Full surrender is necessary to have an abundant life. The fullness of life cannot be experienced without a full surrender, and a full surrender cannot be experienced without fully letting go of the old life. The five issues above could very well be included in the chapter on repentance. However, when receiving Jesus, many do not yet realize all of their sins. This depth of repentance is seldom given any thought early in the Christian walk and by many who confessed Christ a long time ago. But, the Holy Spirit will show you these sins in reading the Bible and in communion with the Lord. In scripture, we notice that repentance, receiving Jesus, water baptism, and Spirit baptism all happen close together. As you grow in Christ, you will discover more ways in which you need to mature and more sin to which you will desire to repent and find release.

After full repentance and surrender to Christ Jesus, you must go on to receive the fullness of the Spirit. Realize that the baptism in the Holy Spirit is a full immersion in the Spirit of God. First, you need to ask, and second, you need to receive in faith. Do as you would in receiving the gift of eternal life; *ask and receive in faith* alone.

> You fathers—if your children ask for a fish, do you give them a snake instead? Or if they ask for an egg, do you give them a scorpion? Of course not! So if you sinful people know how to give good gifts to your children, how much more will your heavenly Father give the Holy Spirit to those who *ask* Him. (Luke 11:11–13; NKJV, my emphasis)

> Through Christ Jesus, God has blessed the Gentiles with the same blessing he promised to Abraham, so that we who are believers might receive the promised Holy Spirit through *faith*. (Gal. 3:14; NKJV, my emphasis).

Notice how we are to ask and receive by faith. Also, notice that believers may receive and that what we receive is the promised Holy Spirit just as it is called in Acts 1 and 2. Remember, Jesus is the baptizer in the Holy Spirit, which He received from the Father when He ascended into heaven, so ask Jesus to baptize you. Do not ask the Holy Spirit to fill or baptize you. Jesus guarantees us that He will give us the promised Holy Spirit when we ask, trusting Him to do it. Whether you have an unusual experience or not makes no difference. It is by believing alone that we receive, not by experience. Do not fear that you will receive something evil. The Bible says that He will not give you a snake or scorpion, which often symbolizes something evil. Believe Him and begin thanking Him. Offer up to Him praise and worship, allowing the Holy Spirit to give you the words which can be in your known language initially, and then let it flow from deep inside your spirit in whatever words the Spirit gives you. Let it flow like rivers of living water, and His presence will be fully experienced. There is nothing like it. Continue in praying like this until the supernatural becomes natural. He loves you and wants this deep fellowship with you. How awesome is that?

Questions to consider:

1. Do you believe God is anxious to baptize you in the Holy Spirit? Read Luke 11:11–13.
2. So how does God react to asking in faith for the promised Holy Spirit?
3. Do you feel or understand the importance of the five steps listed before receiving? Serious repentance is critical for salvation and to avoid conflicting spirits in you.
4. The five steps involve deep repentance that many never heard of before. I would advise all to repent to that level.

CHAPTER 12

PRAYING IN THE SPIRIT

〰〰〰

"I thank God I speak in tongues more than all of you"
(1 Cor. 14:18; NIV).

Praying in the Spirit or praying in tongues was one of my greatest struggles associated with the baptism in the Holy Spirit. In my testimony of receiving the baptism in the Holy Spirit, I shared that I told God that I did not want to speak in tongues when I prayed to receive the pouring out of the Holy Spirit. I had no understanding of the value of this gift and that it is so precious and costly to God. God was so gracious and patient with me in this misunderstanding. I did not have a clear understanding of praying in the Spirit. At the time, there was much negativity concerning praying in the Spirit. People said it was weird, it was from the devil, and it was no longer a functioning gift in our time.

I encountered many different opinions from different people. Quite a few insisted that I did not receive the baptism in the Spirit if I did not speak in tongues. I knew I had, and God supplied plenty of supernatural evidence that I did. Also, the Holy Spirit was giving me many prophetic words, which all came true in detail. Prophecy is also a scriptural sign of the overflow of the

Spirit. Others said I now had the privilege of praying in tongues. So there was confusion that caused me to dig deep into scripture. I was desperate for truth, not opinions. God is so understanding of our lack of understanding. He patiently answered every concern with which I was dealing with concerning speaking in tongues.

In my confusion, I consulted many people concerning praying in tongues. While some claimed that speaking in tongues was the manifestation of having received the baptism in the Holy Spirit, others claimed it no longer happened and was demonic. As I explained in the chapter on receiving the Holy Spirit, calling speaking in tongues demonic is blasphemy of the Holy Spirit. Those who did not experience tongues were negative regardless whether they were spiritual people or not. At one time, the Holy Spirit spoke unexpectedly, saying, "Would you go to an atheist to find out what it is like to be a Christian? Then why would you go to someone inquiring about speaking in tongues, who has never experienced it?" How true. But even some who did speak in tongues left me confused since they could not explain things from scripture. So I still had questions.

One of my primary concerns as I resisted praying in tongues was that not every passage in the book of Acts, which mentioned the baptism in the Holy Spirit, mentioned speaking in tongues. The initial receiving of the Spirit is at Pentecost in Acts chapter 2. There is much detail given here, but I did not think of that as being the definition. I felt that it needed to mention all of the features in each instance following the original. The experience at Pentecost specifically records speaking in at least fifteen languages. With 120 in the upper room, there certainly could have been many more languages spoken because the Bible says all of them were filled with the Holy Spirit and began to speak in other tongues. Notice the word *and*, which means they were all filled with the Spirit and all spoke in tongues. Those hearing heard them speaking the wonders of God (Acts 2:1).

Because of the supernatural manifestation taking place, some thought they had too much to drink. So, Peter got up to explain, saying, these are not drunk as you suppose, but what was happening was the fulfillment of Joel's prophecy in Joel 2:28, 29. To this day, many resist tongues because it looks "far out." It is often called gibberish, even nonsense. The Bible has much to say concerning this gift God designed for His people, as well as the reasons why God, in His infinite wisdom, created such a gift.

Some people who oppose tongues reasoned that the speaking in tongues occurred to get the gospel out to the many languages represented. But here, Peter gets up and speaks to all in their ordinary, everyday language, preaching the gospel. We see that tongues were not used at Pentecost for the gospel to be proclaimed but were a supernatural manifestation of the outpouring of the Holy Spirit as prophesied in scripture. Also, notice verses 17 and 18 point out that all will prophesy. We now have both tongues and prophecy as supernatural evidence of being filled with the Spirit.

Peter's sermon was so powerful that those hearing were cut to the heart and said: "Brothers, what shall we do?" Peter replied, "Repent and let every one of you be baptized in the name of Jesus Christ for the remission of sins, and you shall receive the gift of the Holy Spirit" (Acts 2:37, 38; NKJV). Notice the three instructions that are necessary for each one personally. Each one must repent, each one must be baptized in the name of Jesus Christ for the forgiveness of sins, and each one is commanded to receive the Holy Spirit. This verse does not say that someone else can do any of the three for you, but you need to obey each command personally.

It needs to be pointed out that the phrase which says, "and you shall receive the gift of the Holy Spirit" is not an automatic "shall" but is a command as in the Ten Commandments. Deuteronomy 5:7 says, "You shall have no other gods before me" is an example. Each must personally receive the gift of the Holy Spirit, just like each is to repent personally, and each is to submit to baptism personally; it in no way suggests that another person can do it for you. Personal obedience is consistent with the rest of scripture. The next verse, 39, reads, "For the promise is to you and your children, and to all who are afar off, as many as the Lord our God will call." This verse is often pulled out of context and misused.

First, notice the words, "the promise." If you read Acts 1 and 2, observe the use of the phrase *"the promise"* in 1:4 and 2:33 are clearly about the baptism of the Holy Spirit and not something else like water baptism. "To you and your children" means to those who were listening, Jews, and those living in Jerusalem. "Their children," in this case, means descendants regardless of age. It does not mean infants or little children. The phrase *far off* means Gentiles, as explained in Ephesians 2 and 3, where those near refer to Jews. This verse in context is for the reception of the gift of the Holy Spirit. It is for Jews and Gentiles, those near, the Jews, and those far away, the Gentiles. It does not mean infant baptism as some denominations use it.

The second incident of receiving the Holy Spirit is of the Samaritans in Chapter 8. Here Philip presented the gospel performing many miraculous signs of casting out demons and with many healings (verses 4–8). Those who believed Philip as he preached the good news of the kingdom of God were baptized. "When the apostles in Jerusalem heard that Samaria had accepted the word of God, they sent Peter and John to them." When they arrived, they prayed for them that they might receive the Holy Spirit. Notice again that the receiving of the Holy Spirit came after they believed and were baptized. There was a definite lapse of time since they had been baptized in water and receiving the gift of the Holy Spirit. They didn't receive the Holy Spirit until after Peter and John arrived. There is no mention of speaking in tongues here. However, what did Simon see when the Holy Spirit was given when the apostles laid hands on people, which caused him to offer money for such an ability? It was not the miracles Philip performed earlier and witnessed by Simon, but something was recognized when he laid hands on them, and people received the Holy Spirit that caused him to offer money for the gift. Could it have been the same manifestation as in Acts 2? There is no other option.

Moving to Acts 9, we have the third time someone received the Holy Spirit; it was when Saul was converted on the way to Damascus. After Saul and Ananias both had a vision and were given instruction by the Holy Spirit, they met at the house of Judas. Ananias went into the house and placed his hands on Saul and said:

> Brother Saul, the Lord—Jesus, who appeared to; you on the road as you were coming here—has sent me so that you may see again and be filled with the Holy Spirit. Immediately, something like scales fell from Saul's eyes, and he could see again. He got up and was baptized, and after taking some food, he regained his strength. (Acts 9:17–19; NIV)

Saul had repented, received Jesus, was baptized, healed, and was filled with the Holy Spirit. Here is another incident that speaking in tongues is not mentioned, but we know from 1 Corinthians 14:18 that Saul, now Paul, spoke in tongues and taught extensively on the subject. Paul gives more detail to his testimony in Acts 22:1–16 as he was providing his defense.

Not only had the Holy Spirit been given to the Samaritans, but in Acts 10, we have the fourth account of the Gentiles receiving the Holy Spirit. Knowing how Jews felt about Gentiles in that day makes this a story of high drama. Cornelius was a Gentile, and Jews were forbidden to enter Gentile houses. However, after a vision, Peter went into the house. Cornelius, along with his relatives and close friends, were eagerly waiting for Peter to share with them. Peter began to share and explain Jesus's ministry to them.

> While Peter was still speaking, the Holy Spirit came on all who heard the message. The circumcised believers who had come with Peter were astonished that the gift of the Holy Spirit had been poured out even on the Gentiles. For they heard them speaking in tongues and praising God. Then Peter said, "Surely no one can stand in the way of their being baptized with water? They have received the Holy Spirit just as we have." So he ordered that they be baptized in the name of Jesus Christ. (Acts 10:44–48; NIV)

The story of Cornelius is such a great story because we now know that the gift of the Holy Spirit as it happened on Pentecost is for all people, including Samaritans and Gentiles, which includes me. Peter did get "called on the carpet" for his actions, as we see in Acts 11 and defended his actions.

> As I began to speak, the Holy Spirit came on them as he had come on us at the beginning. Then I remembered what the Lord had said: 'John baptized with water, but you will be baptized with the Holy Spirit.' So if God gave them the same gift as he gave us, who believed in the Lord Jesus Christ,

who was I to think that I could stand in God's way?
(Acts 11:15–17; NIV)

There were no further objections to his actions; in fact, they praised God for giving this powerful gift along with forgiveness of sins to the Gentiles also. This story took place six to eight years after Pentecost.

Paul was not one of the twelve, but in Chapter 13, Paul began his ministry. Paul continued his ministry in the same way and the same pattern as Peter and John. In Acts 19:1–7, we have the fifth incident of Spirit baptism as Paul arrives at Ephesus and his first question for the believers was: "Did you receive the Holy Spirit when you believed?" (Acts 19:2; NIV).

If receiving the Holy Spirit was automatic when you believed, this question would certainly not be asked. Consider the seriousness of that question. It is the inspired Word of God. We all need to answer the question. Have you received the Holy Spirit when you believed? They answered, "No, we have not even heard that there is a Holy Spirit," so they positively could not have received Him. So Paul asked, "Then what baptism did you receive?" That question, combined with asking if they received the Holy Spirit, indicates that Paul was not speaking of when one is born of the Holy Spirit, but the real question being asked was, did you receive the baptism in the Holy Spirit when you believed? The answer to that is they never heard of it. So when asked what baptism did you receive, they replied, "John's baptism," which was water baptism. Paul replied, "John's baptism was a baptism of repentance. John the Baptist told the people to believe in the one coming after him, that is, in Jesus." On hearing Paul's explanation, they were baptized in water again, this time in the name of the Lord Jesus Christ. Then Paul placed his hands on them, the Holy Spirit came on them, and they spoke in tongues and prophesied. Acts 19 takes place about nineteen years after Pentecost, showing that receiving the gift of the Holy Spirit continued after Pentecost.

There are two places in the book of Acts that do not mention speaking in tongues when the baptism of the Holy Spirit took place. However, as I said, in the case of Paul, we do know that he spoke in tongues. As he states in 1 Corinthians 14:18, "I thank God that I speak in tongues more than all of you." That leaves only one incident, which was the Samaritans receiving the baptism in the Holy Spirit where tongues were not mentioned. However, the question of what did Simon see that made him desire strongly the power to lay hands on others so they would receive the baptism in the Holy Spirit needs an answer. He already saw the mighty miracles performed by the apostles. So by elimination, there was only one thing left, and that was speaking in tongues which Simon witnessed and desired power to confer.

In some way, I still thought that speaking in tongues was optional. The gift of tongues was mentioned last in the list in 1 Corinthians 12:28, so the prevailing belief was that it was the least significant. I went on thinking for months that the speaking in tongues was not substantial, nor was it necessary. I did not realize the benefits because I never experienced it. It would be like asking someone who has never been born of the Spirit, what it is like to be born again. The Holy Spirit would not let me get by, reasoning that way. There was a stronghold against my willingness to receiving a prayer language. Would God offer gifts that have little useful-lness? The Holy Spirit continued gently leading me to the truth.

One day while in my devotion time, the Holy Spirit spoke to me clearly, "If you paid a high price for a gift for one of your children, and when you presented it to them, they said, 'I really do not see the value of this, and therefore I would not use it, so just keep it,' how would I feel?" Terrible! At that time, I realized how vital speaking in tongues was to God and how much He desires it for all His children. At another time, the Spirit said to me, "When you are teaching about isosceles triangles (triangles with at least two equal sides), do you go through all the details about isosceles triangles every time you teach about them? Or, in time, do you expect the students to know the details?" Immediately I knew that all the details of the baptism in the Holy Spirit and speaking in tongues are mentioned enough times and that it would be repetitive to repeat it each time. The gift must be of great value for His children if He paid so much for us to have it. The Bible explains, "He took the curse when He hung on a tree that we might receive the promised Holy Spirit" (Gal. 3:13, 14; NKJV). Jesus was hung on the cross so we could receive the promised Holy Spirit? That's an incredible price. Why would anyone not want such an expensive gift?

As I began to see the gentle and loving persistence of the Spirit, convicting and convincing me, my defenses went down. It was October 10, 1971, when I gave my life to the Lord, and it was March 5, 1973, when I received the baptism in the Holy Spirit. One evening in the summer of 1974, our Bible study group of which I was a part, went for a ride to the river. One of the guys wanted to stop by the river just west of Hospers to visit the place he had been baptized. He wanted to be alone to reflect, so we each went off in different directions along the river.

I went out into a pasture where there were some trees. One tree had some low branches, enabling me to climb up into it. I found a comfortable position to sit on a limb and began to pray for the gift of a private prayer language. By this time, fully believing a prayer language was God's will for me, and like anyone baptized in the Holy Spirit, I began worshipping and praising God, requesting a prayer language. After some time about three strange words came out; that was all.

That continued for weeks with the same words every time. I began to wonder if the few words I continued to speak were the real deal. There was no clear teaching around to offer an authentic, spiritual understanding. I depended entirely on the Word of God, the voice of the Lord, and the Holy Spirit to provide clarity and understanding. These same words seemed to come for quite some time, perhaps months.

One evening as my wife, Fran, and I headed south out of town, we came upon a head-on collision involving a full-sized car and a Volkswagen Beatle. We were the second car on the scene. I said, "We need to stop and see if we can help." The small car did not fare well in the head-on collision and had five people in it. The Volkswagen ended up in a deep ditch on all four wheels, pointing in the opposite direction of travel. The front of the small car was flat to the front seat, and both passengers in the front seat were dead. There were three boys in the back seat. The sound coming from that car as a result of the severe pain was unequal to anything I have ever heard. The compassion I felt for the people was massive, causing me to pray. I placed my hand on top of the vehicle above the back seat, and unknown words flowed out freely from deep within me. After the emergency vehicles arrived and bodies were removed from the car, one of the EMTs, who was a former student, called out, "Mr. Vermeer, you have to come here and help me." I went over to her, and she told me how to hold the boy's head so she could perform other tasks to prepare him for the ambulance. His brains were protruding out of his forehead. At that sight, my spirit was so moved that the unknown words just poured out again.

My understanding was that with such an injury where the brain was exposed, a person would not survive. I carefully followed the news concerning the boy I helped and prayed over. To my surprise, he was alive and in a hospital in Sioux City. I drove up to see him in the intensive care unit and spoke with a nurse, explaining who I was and what had happened. She took me to the boy in the ICU. The boy's head was bandaged entirely, so I could not see his face. She said it was a miracle the boy was even alive and didn't know how he would turn out. Sometime later, I read in the Sioux City paper that he was dismissed from the hospital and returned to school. In addition to the vigorous stirring in my spirit, which caused the unknown words to pour out, an incredible miracle occurred, demonstrating the power of praying in the Spirit.

I now understood what the Bible said in 1 Corinthians 14:14, "If I pray in a tongue, my spirit prays, but my mind is unfruitful." It originated in my spirit, my innermost being, because of the indwelling Holy Spirit living in my spirit, my innermost being, or my heart. I needed to speak, but the Spirit within my spirit produced the language that I didn't know. I soon discovered that it is not necessary to experience an almost heart-stopping incident as I experienced at the scene of the accident for a rising up of your spirit to speak in an unknown tongue. The Lord used that experience to help me get started praying in the spirit. I had to learn that it originates deep in your spirit, and I needed to let it flow from there, but I needed to speak. After some experience, I was able to begin any time speaking and trusting the Holy Spirit to form the words. In a short time, it would be effortless to let it flow from my innermost being. Receiving it in faith is vital. The Bible says in Galatians 3:14 (NLT), "so that we who are believers might receive the promised Holy Spirit through faith." Also, the Bible says in Luke 11:13 (NLT), "So if you sinful people know how to give good gifts to your children, how much more will your heavenly Father give the Holy Spirit to those who ask him." I needed to *ask* and *receive* in faith.

I was making praying in the spirit much more complicated than necessary. I would almost get turned off by people who said,

"Just do it." With some understanding, it is about that simple. I was thinking God was to do everything, not realizing that I had a part in receiving the gift by speaking in faith, and the Spirit's role was to provide the language. I had to speak, permitting the words to come from my spirit, and the Holy Spirit provides the words supernaturally. It is as simple as receiving salvation through faith. You believe, you ask, and you receive. It is like Jesus says in Luke 11:9–10 (NLT), "And so I tell you, keep on asking, and you will receive what you ask for. Keep on seeking, and you will find. Keep on knocking, and the door will be opened to you. For everyone who asks, receives. Everyone who seeks finds. And to everyone who knocks, the door will be opened."

The Bible provides additional information about praying in tongues. First Corinthians 14:2 states that we are speaking to God; since people will not be able to understand, it will be a mystery to man. Verse 4 says, "A person who speaks in a tongue is strengthened personally." We certainly need edification personally. When speaking in tongues, you may be speaking in tongues of men or angels. There are many languages and dialects in the world from many tribes and nations. There have been times when someone has understood someone speaking in tongues like at Pentecost. One hundred and twenty were speaking in tongues, and about fifteen languages were recognized.

It is essential to understand the context of 1 Corinthians, chapter 14. Notice that the instructions given are while in the church gathering. If a person prays in the spirit out loud in a church assemble, interpretation should follow. If an interpreter is not present, the person should pray in tongues silently. First Corinthians 11–14 is about corporate worship in a church setting. So when it says in verse 12:30, "all do not speak in tongues, do they" has the obvious answer—no, since only two or three should pray in tongues in a gathering. That is to be understood as in a church meeting; however, in private, we can all speak in tongues. In private, I encourage everyone to pray in tongues out loud. Praying in the spirit is powerful and very effective. It is mighty in spiritual warfare because the Holy Spirit is providing the words. Since the powers of darkness cannot read your mind, spiritual warfare prayer needs to be prayed out loud. Always pray out loud when taking authority over evil. Interpretation is not necessary if used to worship and praise God as an entire assembly. Nor is interpretation essential if it used for intercession in private prayer. I have discovered praying in tongues privately certainly does edify or build myself up, primarily when used for an extended period, like half an hour or more. It is a way to pray without ceasing. Edification often comes later rather than simultaneously.

Private praying in tongues is powerful and is in the perfect will of the Father. The Bible says in Romans 8:26–27 (NLT):

> And the Holy Spirit helps us in our weakness. For example, we don't know what God wants us to pray for. But the Holy Spirit prays for us with groanings that cannot be expressed in words. And the Father who knows all hearts knows what the Spirit is saying, for the Spirit pleads for us believers in harmony with God's own will.

All Spirit-filled believers have this ability. The question in 1 Corinthians 12:30, "Do we all have the ability to speak in unknown languages?" has the obvious answer, "Of course not!" The application to all these questions is in the assembly of believers and not in private. But in private, Paul says, "I thank God that I speak in tongues more than all of you" (1 Cor. 14:18). How could such a gift be inferior as I once thought?

Praying in tongues is always praying in the perfect will of God. There cannot be a more powerful prayer. Private praying in unknown languages builds one up in faith and intimacy with the Lord. The fellowship with the Lord increases dramatically, even to the point of overwhelming a person. If continued for a certain length of time, depending on personal sensitivity to the Spirit, praying in the power of the Holy Spirit is extremely edifying. Praying in the Spirit will usher you into the holy presence of God. We are allowing the Spirit to flood our spirit and soul with His presence, producing joy and peace not possible by praying only with the understanding, that is, with the mind.

I'll give just one example of praying in the power of the Holy Spirit. One day when my son and his family were living in Iowa City, my son called concerning his son, my grandson, who was in the hospital with a bowel obstruction that needed to be solved immediately. The hospital in Iowa City had a noninvasive procedure to eliminate the blockage. The method was attempted unsuccessfully three times, which was the limit. My son, with a quiver in his voice, called, asking for prayer. Upon hanging up, I immediately lifted my hands toward Iowa City and began to pray in the Spirit because I didn't know how to pray. The doctor was inspired to try one more time, and the procedure worked, eliminating the obstruction. To some, that just happened, but I believe it was the power of prayer. There have been many other times that praying in tongues resulted in a miracle. The father of lies will tell us otherwise. The Bible says that it is "Not by might nor by power, but by my Spirit says the Lord Almighty" (Zech. 4:6; NIV).

Paul makes an incredible statement in 1 Corinthians 14:18 (NIV). "I thank God that I speak in tongues more than any of you." If you read the next sentence, you will understand Paul means in private. Paul prays in the Spirit frequently. Praying in tongues is so powerful and beneficial to the man who wrote much of the New

Testament. It is equally powerful and advantageous to each of us. "Do not forbid speaking in other tongues" (1 Cor. 14:39; NLT).

Jesus also made an astounding statement when he said in John 16:7 (NLT), "It is best for you that I go away because if I don't, the Advocate (the Holy Spirit) won't come." Jesus said that to his disciple who walked with Him about three and a half years, listening to His teachings and seeing incredible signs, wonders, and miracles that He performed. Could anything be better than that? Jesus said the receiving of the Holy Spirit is better. If Jesus made such a statement concerning the coming of the Holy Spirit at Pentecost, why would anyone not strongly desire the baptism in the Holy Spirit with the biblical manifestation of speaking in tongues and prophesying? Do you have such a desire? Ask and receive the gift in faith.

Questions to consider:

1. Praying in the Spirit has many practical purposes. Have you ever considered it to develop intimacy with the Lord?
2. Did you understand that you have a part as well as the Holy Spirit in praying in the Spirit?
3. Do you understand the power of praying in the Holy Spirit?
4. Can you list some of the benefits of praying in tongues?
5. Would God give gifts of little significance?

CHAPTER 13

SIGNS, WONDERS, AND MIRACLES

⚜

(Gifts of the Holy Spirit)

"And God confirmed the message by giving signs and wonders and various miracles and gifts of the Holy Spirit whenever he chose" (Heb. 2:4; NLT).

T he Hebrews 2:4 verse shows God confirmed the gospel message by signs, wonders, and miracles. Jesus's ministry also confirmed the message. Notice the ongoing pattern. Jesus sent out the twelve with the instructions to drive out demons, cure diseases, and heal the sick. After that, Jesus sent out the seventy-two with the same directions, and before His ascension, He gave the Great Commission, recorded in Matthew and Mark; and telling them miraculous signs would accompany them. Miracles confirmed their teaching and preaching. Without the teaching and preaching of the Word, there would have been little reason for the wonders. (The Holy Spirit just pointed out to me as I am writing to notice the two go together, so people would both see and hear the gospel.) The Spirit worked through the words spoken, bringing much conviction, cutting to the heart. But, God also confirmed the message by signs, wonders, and miracles. The apostles saw and heard the ministry of Jesus and followed His example as Jesus commanded.

The apostles, Peter and John, said as they were on trial before the Sanhedrin, 'For we cannot help speaking about what we have seen and heard" (Acts 4:19; NIV). Notice that both senses of seeing and hearing are used. Jesus referred to the same two reasons when John the Baptist sent his disciples to inquire if Jesus was the one who is to come. Jesus replied, "Go back and report to John what you hear and see" (Matt. 11:4 NIV). The apostle Paul said, "My message and my preaching were not with wise and persuasive words, but with a demonstration of the Spirit's power" (1 Cor. 2:4; NIV). If one is on the alert for it, you will notice both seeing and hearing are mentioned often in scripture and, therefore, necessary for maximum effectiveness in sharing the gospel.

We notice the same in the teachings of Jesus as He prepared the disciples to continue His ministry. Initially, He sent out the twelve and commanded them to make way for Jesus. "When Jesus had called the Twelve together, He gave them power and authority to drive out all demons and to cure diseases, and he sent them out to proclaim the kingdom of God and to heal the sick" (Luke 9:1, 2; NIV).

In the next chapter, Luke 10, Jesus sends out seventy-two other messengers. He gives detailed instructions on what to do and what to say. Jesus commanded them as follows: "Heal the sick who are there and tell them, 'The kingdom of God is near you'" (Luke 10:9; NIV). The command of Jesus again includes both what to do and what to say. The next assignment is the Great Commission Jesus gives to all believers. First the twelve, then the seventy-two, and now all believers are sent out to witness. Notice that Jesus gives power and authority to those He sends out.

> Then Jesus came to them and said, "All authority in heaven and on earth has been given to me. Therefore go and make disciples of all nations, baptizing them in the name of the Father and of the Son and of the Holy Spirit, and teaching them to obey everything I have commanded you. And surely I am with you always to the very end of the age." (Matt. 28:18–20 NIV)

Immediately after the Great Commission, in Acts 1:4–8, Jesus commands them first to wait until they are baptized in the Holy Spirit to receive the power to be His witnesses to the ends of the earth. They waited and prayed ten days, from the ascension to Pentecost. There were about one hundred and twenty gathered on Pentecost when they were all filled with the Holy Spirit. After they were filled with the Holy Spirit and Peter preached to the crowd they attracted, three thousand were added to their number. Notice how quickly the gospel spread and multiplied when the Spirit is poured out in power. Now all who repented and received Christ were baptized, filled with the Holy Spirit, and were obeying the Great Commission. Likewise, now all who believe are to be witnesses bringing the gospel to a lost and hurting world as they did in the beginning.

Jesus fully intends for us to follow Him in building the kingdom. In John chapter seventeen, Jesus not only prays for the twelve but for all who believe their message in the future. "My prayer is not for them alone. I also pray for those who will believe in me through their message" (John 17:20; NIV).

Preceding this prayer are Jesus's instructions concerning the working of the Holy Spirit, recorded in John chapters 14, 15, and 16. There are incredible promises in these chapters for obedient followers of Jesus. These are not vending-machine promises for anyone, believer or nonbeliever, but are for all who are genuinely in love with Jesus. For genuine followers of Jesus, He makes astonishing promises.

> I tell you the truth, anyone who has faith in me will do what I have been doing. He will do even greater things than these, because I am going to the Father. And I will do whatever you ask in my name, so that the Son may bring glory to the Father. You may ask me for anything in my name, and I will do it. (John 14:12–14; NIV)

Some say, "If God heals or delivers me, then I will believe." But notice in this verse, faith precedes the miracles, not the other way around. If it begins with faith, where does such faith originate? It originates in the heart of the believer who has wholly surrendered their heart to Christ; faith comes from hearing the Word, resulting in personal knowledge of Christ. Faith must be placed in Jesus, who is the object of our faith. In Acts 6:5, Stephen, a man full of faith and the Holy Spirit, was chosen as a deacon. In verse 8, it says that "Stephen, a man full of God's grace and power, did great wonders and miraculous signs among the people."

"Receiving the Holy Spirit as in the beginning" will quicken faith. The gift of the Holy Spirit stirs up confidence in the heart where faith originates. There is a reason Jesus spent much time teaching on the Holy Spirit. He knew the filling of the Holy Spirit to be critical for any disciple to go out in following Jesus. Signs and wonders and various kinds of miracles and gifts of the Holy

Spirit are for the building of the kingdom so that people will both hear and see the greatness of the Lord. The gifts of the Holy Spirit will also illuminate the follower of Jesus, creating greater boldness in sharing the gospel.

Personal Experiences

I have seen many miracles and healings in my walk with the Lord. One of the earliest miracles I can recall was shortly after receiving the baptism in the Holy Spirit. Our son, Dan, who was very young at the time, maybe three or four, was in the backyard playing with another little neighbor boy. They were playing with a golf club and swinging pretty hard at a golf ball. I was watching out of the window, thinking I need to warn them to be more careful when at the same time, the neighbor boy swung the club just as my son reached to pick up the ball, which was next to a young tree. My son got his finger between the club and the tree, smashing his finger.

He immediately started crying hard and ran around to the front of the house. As he entered the house crying, his mother, Fran, and I began tending to his finger and trying to comfort him as best as possible as it had to really hurt him. After caring for him, it was time for our evening meal. We always prayed out loud before eating, and as I was praying, I felt the Spirit nudging me to pray for his finger. I asked the Lord to heal Dan's finger. After we finished praying, Dan looked at me and said, "Dad, look at my finger." I looked, and it was completely healed with only a tiny piece of loose skin left. As bad as his finger looked, there was no doubt this was supernatural.

Another miracle happened near the same time, shortly after I received the gift of the Holy Spirit. We had an old, second-hand car that I used to drive to do things like going to town and the city dump. One time I brought garbage to the dump and stopped the car to unload my trash, and when I tried to start it, it didn't do anything. I prayed about the situation and asked God to help in starting the old car. When I tried it again, it started right up, and I went home, thinking it just happened that it started. However, the next time I was going to use it, it didn't start again. I remembered the last time I prayed, and it started, so I thought, I'll try that again. I prayed, and it started. I got uptown, did my business, and it would not start again. I repeated praying for the car to start, and it did.

I realized something had to be wrong, so I took it to a gas station, and at that time, they fixed and serviced cars as well as sold gas. A serviceman looked at it, and there was a cable-like wire that connected to the battery, which was hanging there, completely disconnected. The serviceman said that it could not only start but couldn't even run without that wire connected, and I just drove it down to the station. The mechanic repaired the wire, and the car started without prayer. That story may sound a bit strange, but God performed an undeniable miracle. The impossible is possible with God.

Why would God perform such a miracle? It was so different from healing, which would benefit a person physically and emotionally. Perhaps one might ask the same question of Jesus changing water into wine. Or, how would walking on water benefit anyone? Why would Jesus perform such miracles? Assuredly, it would prove that He was the Son of God. It also demonstrated His power over everything, all of which He created by speaking into being. Yes, He is great and greatly to be praised. He cares about every detail in our lives. He is a loving God, and so much more.

For several years we held an outreach service at our church on Sunday afternoons. We would pray for people with all kinds of requests at any of the services. Also, we included a designated healing service every two or three months. There were many answers to prayer as we obeyed scripture. I recall two seriously ill men who received prayer, both giving testimony of supernatural healing.

I was often involved in praying for others; however, there were instances where I also requested prayer. One time, I fell very hard on my back on an icy sidewalk, causing much pain that persisted. I tried several things, including physical therapy, and nothing relieved the pain in my back. Finally, the doctor ordered x-rays of my back, and they discovered a fractured vertebra. Another healing service was scheduled at our outreach service. I always attended, and that night I wanted prayer for my back. We had several stations around the perimeter of the chapel, each occupied by a team of two prayer people. People could go to any station they desired.

One man successfully prayed for back problems in several people. Therefore, I was determined to go to him, but he was continuously busy, and the service was soon to end. So I went to another team, was anointed with oil, and they prayed over me. I felt nothing, such as tingling or heat or any other manifestation while they prayed for me. I returned to my seat, and my back was feeling remarkably good as I sat very straight in my chair, thinking it would ease any pain. Initially, I thought it was the chair nicely fitting my back, providing the relief. But, as I drove home, I felt no pain. I had no pain at home and no pain in bed the entire night. By the time I got up in the morning, I had realized that my back was pain-free regardless of position or movement. I realized I was healed.

The Monday morning after the healing service, I had another appointment with physical therapy. I went in and told the therapist that I went to a healing service the previous night, they prayed over me, and I was healed. I got a strange look and a doubtful smile. The therapist worked with me and said that she wanted me back one more time to see how I was progressing. I asked for an x-ray to prove I was healed, but they said they could not allow it since the insurance would not pay for it when there was no pain. I returned in two days, and they again examined me and agreed there was no problem regardless of the various movements they performed. They dismissed me. Jesus healed me through the power of the Holy Spirit.

I have prayed for people in various places, including hospitals, in church, in the backyard, in the garage, anyplace someone tells me about an illness. All I needed to do was ask if I could pray for them. I never had anyone turn me down. In obedience, I saw the Lord do many remarkable things. I also had instances where nothing seemed to happen. We must understand there are many reasons why healing doesn't take place. The Bible gives over thirty reasons why healing does not occur. Perhaps the most frequently mentioned blocks to healing are lack of forgiveness and unbelief.

The gifts of knowledge, wisdom, and prophecy are extremely helpful in enabling another in receiving a gift of healing. Notice that Jesus, having all knowledge, always got right to the precise point and was one hundred percent successful. Only through the gifts of the Holy Spirit can we approach such success. Jesus was filled with the Holy Spirit without limit in all the gifts of the Holy Spirit, but we are partial and incomplete in giftedness. Regardless of the outcome, Jesus commanded us to pray for others. "Now our knowledge is partial and incomplete, and even the gift of prophecy reveals only part of the whole picture! But when the time of perfection comes, these partial things will become useless" (1 Cor. 13:9, 10; NLT).

The time of perfection is when the perfect one returns.

I share a story of how a word of knowledge enhanced the working of a miracle. I was on staff in our church, and I received a call from an elderly lady whose grandson was in a severe condition from a fall from a tractor. The lady was a member of our church but not the rest of the family, who some years before were members but had moved away. She had four children, one son and three daughters. Two of the daughters were part of the group of students involved in praying for me to give my life to Christ. As a result, I was close to the family since they always took a spiritual interest in me. As I was traveling to Sioux Falls to make the call, I asked God for a special favor for this family who meant so much to me since they were involved in my conversion. While traveling and praying, the Spirit gave this word of knowledge, "If you lay one finger on the boy, I will heal him."

I arrived and visited briefly with the family since I had not seen them for some time. They explained the seriousness of the boy's condition as he was barely hanging on to life. After visiting, the lady's son, who was the father of the boy and myself, went to the ICU to see him. The boy's head was bandaged entirely, except for one little spot large enough to touch him with the tip of one finger. Now it was apparent what the Spirit meant by placing one finger on him; it was all I could do. Due to his condition, I offered a very brief prayer for his healing as I laid one finger on the open spot. Later he recovered and went home, healed by the Spirit. Hallelujah! God loves to heal.

My inclination is that as God begins to pour out the latter rains of the Spirit, the final outpouring of the Spirit, the gifts of the Holy Spirit will significantly increase. The Lord will speak frequently and reveal unusual knowledge and revelations of things to come. Such an outpouring will be for those who are intimate and fully dedicated to the Lord. Many will both see and hear, some with understanding. "Those who are wise will shine like the brightness of the heavens, and those who lead many to righteousness, like the stars forever and ever" (Dan. 12:3; NIV).

Healing and miracles happen in ways we do not always understand. Sometimes they are instantaneous and with unusual manifestations. Sometimes the healing seems to come slowly. We need to remember that the church has been very inactive in ministering the gifts of the Holy Spirit and in the knowledge of the Holy Spirit for centuries and is, in many instances, in complete denial. We have many blocks in our minds, having believed the lies of the evil one. The evil one does not want us to have such knowledge. Satan has set up strategies well ahead of our time to discourage and block our understanding of the working of miracles. If we don't see signs and wonders right away, we believe that God no longer does them because that would have a reflection of weakness on us. But, God will raise a standard against the enemy and his lies, pouring out His Spirit with fresh knowledge and revelation. It is already beginning to occur worldwide.

I share one more of the many miracles I have experienced. This miracle happened in my body, and I admit I do not fully understand when this healing happened. I was at the dentist for an annual cleaning of my teeth when the technician observed a spot on my tongue and asked the dentist to look at it when he came in to check my teeth. After he looked it over, he felt I should go to an ENT (ear, nose, and throat doctor). I made an appointment with an ENT doctor, and he thought it was all right but would need semiannual check-ups to follow it, which we did for several years.

After that time of several years, I was leading a search team for a pastor for our church. I led the team on a retreat at Willow Creek Church in a Chicago suburb. We were there for a weekend, praying and seeking the Lord's leading in finding a pastor. I experienced a sharp pain in the spot on my tongue, which was under observation by the ENT. When we returned on Monday, I immediately went to my family doctor. He suggested I see a dermatologist, which seemed very strange to me since the spot was inside of my mouth and not on the outer skin. I questioned the decision, but the doctor insisted that a dermatologist will see it differently than an ENT. When the dermatologist took one brief look at it, he said, "That has to come off immediately, and an ENT must do it because if I biopsy it, I will mess it up for the ENT."

I immediately returned to my family doctor who was suspicious about the spot, and he now asked, "Where would you like to go?" Not knowing what to say so quickly, nor did I suspect anything real serious, I said, "What do you think of the Mayo Clinic?" Without a response, he picked up the phone and called for an appointment. Anyone who has not been to Mayo before cannot get in immediately. I would have to wait to get an appointment since they were not willing to admit me right away. My doctor did not receive any excuse from the scheduler and strongly insisted I be accepted. Finally, I had to be there in less than four hours when it was a four-hour drive from Sioux Center to Rochester, Minnesota. First, I went home as fast as possible, threw a few clothes in a carry-on case, and left with my wife. We needed to go over the speed limit to get there in three and a half hours, which we did.

I was examined by the head of the ENT department and a couple of other doctors. As a team, they didn't think it was severe but would remove it and set up an appointment for surgery in a week. We went home and returned in a week for the operation. At the initial visit, they already warned me that I would need some speech therapy following surgery on my tongue. Needing speech therapy was a concern to me because I was singing on the praise team in church. Worship in the church was a significant concern to me as I had been praying for years to see genuine worship, and it was finally beginning. I desired everyone to have the experience of coming into the presence of the Lord through worship, especially in my church. My prayer was that I would be able to continue serving in that capacity. I didn't think the removal of a spot on my tongue would be a big problem.

They prepped me for surgery and placed me in the holding area to go into surgery that morning since I was squeezed in the schedule. The operation was to be a same-day surgery. After surgery, when I was in recovery, I should not have been able to speak, and especially not clearly. I remember talking in words which I, nor others, understood as I was praying in the spirit. While I was under the influence of drugs from general anesthesia, I drifted in and out, remembering some things. I remember waking and speaking clearly the words, "Will I still be able to praise God in the sanctuary?" Upon hearing that, the nurse attending me burst into tears and quickly left. I remember another nurse coming to my aid, and then I drifted off to sleep again.

After being fully awake, the doctors explained that there was cancer in my tongue and that they removed tissue until they had clear margins. The cancer identified was squamous cell carcinoma. I was told the name, which didn't mean a lot to me. We were not informed of the seriousness of this type of cancer inside the mouth. They told me that they removed about a two-inch moon-shaped piece to a depth near the center of my tongue. They explained that I would need speech therapy to learn how to speak with my deformed tongue.

At first, they had me come back frequently for check-ups and put me on a drug, not chemo, for six months. The word *cancer* never affected me that much. I was not worried about it for some reason. On one of the early check-ups to Rochester, as we were making our four-hour trip down Interstate 90, I plugged in a Promise Keepers cassette tape. As I entered into worship, the presence of the Lord filled the car. I was unaware of anything for miles, overwhelmed by His presence. I was driving, at least I was behind the steering wheel, perhaps not the best thing, but His presence came all over me. It was an awesome time with the Lord, and the only thing I knew was Jesus's presence. It was intense, and I was full of joy, with perfect peace about everything.

My tongue grew back and filled in so quickly that I never did need speech therapy. I did have to return frequently for check-ups. As time went on, I did not have to go for check-ups as often. When I hit the three-year mark, which I understood to be the critical point, I went down from every six months to eventually once a year for check-ups. At the end of six years, they dismissed me.

All the while, I had the head of the ENT department, Dr. Kasperbauer, examine me for my check-ups. At the end of that time, I asked Dr. Kasperbauer, "Just how serious was this deal?" He looked me in the eyes and said, "If one cell had gotten by, you would have been dead in three years." Then he said, "Someone was watching over you." I replied, "And I know who." He said, "So do I." Later as I returned to my family doctor explaining that I had been dismissed, he said, "Someone was watching over you." He used the same words as the doctor at Mayo used. He also said, "I know who was watching over you." Amazing affirmation!

In speaking with the doctors and asking questions about this form of cancer, they said it is perilous in the mouth. They told me that there is a tiny window of time between the appearance of the spot and its becoming malignant and spreading. The doctor said to me that catching it inside that small window of time would be a greater miracle than an outright gift of healing. Surgery capturing this type of cancer over such a long time in just the right moment would be impossible. In this case, clear margins didn't mean that surgery eliminated cancer. Since that time, I have heard of this type of cancer in the mouth quite often and have not heard of one survivor. That is why the doctors said, "Someone was watching over you." There was cancer in the pathology report, and now it is no more.

The miracle was apparent whether the doctors just happened to catch it in that tiny window of time out of several years in dealing with the spot on my tongue or if the healing was miraculous. Considering the length of time I had the spot on my tongue, the probability of catching it at precisely the right time is near zero. But, when and how the miracle took place, I do not know. I had never requested prayer for healing by others or prayed for healing myself, and I do not know when or how it happened. I had complete trust in the Father that the Holy Spirit gave me. If I were to guess when healing took place, I would pick the time when I was traveling to Rochester, and the Spirit of God came all over me in the car. I do not believe cancer could stay in my body when such a formidable presence of the Lord came over me. Whatever happened, God selected the most excellent way. The perfect way is when you never have to deal with it; no chemo and no radiation.

Jesus is our example for everything, including healing. The four gospels record the "job description" of Jesus several times. The first general description of the ministry of Jesus is in Matthew 4:23–24 (NIV):

> Jesus went throughout Galilee, teaching in their synagogues, preaching the good news of the Kingdom, and healing every disease and sickness among the people. News about him spread all over Syria, and people brought to him all who were ill with various diseases, those suffering severe pain, the demon-possessed, those having seizures, and the paralyzed, and he healed them.

There are three more similar descriptions in Matthew of the ministry of Jesus. There are more just like it in the other gospels. It is clear why Jesus came. The Father sent Jesus to undo the works of Satan, paving the way for the restoration of the Kingdom upon his second coming. "You know what has happened throughout Judea, beginning in Galilee after the baptism that John preached—how God anointed Jesus of Nazareth with the Holy Spirit and power, and how he went around doing good and healing all who were under the power of the devil, because God was with him" (Acts 10:37, 38; NIV).

Why did Jesus do all of those mighty miracles? It says He did them to undo the works of Satan. Illnesses are from Satan. Another reason is that Jesus had great compassion and love for the people. Even though the fall of humankind and sin brought about all of our troubles, God still loves people as He did when He created Adam and Eve and placed them in the beautiful Garden of Eden. God is love forever and ever. He is unchanging. When we believe God doesn't care and doesn't love us, we have been sold a bunch of lies from the father of lies. We need to come back to the teaching of the apostles and Jesus.

He also performed supernatural acts so people could both see and hear the gospel, the good news. He did such works to draw people to Himself for evangelism. As one reads through the book of Acts, we witness high numbers of people coming to the Lord, three thousand on the first day. We continue to see significant numbers of people giving their lives to Jesus through the preaching of the Word, and even higher numbers come when signs, wonders, and miracles are performed through the hands of evangelists.

The same is still true today. Consider the ministry of the late Reinhard Bonnke, as seventy-seven million in Africa were saved as signs, wonders, and miracles accompanied his lifetime of preaching. I had observed people running to the alter when the call was given. Miracles significantly increase the effectiveness of the teaching of the Word as those watching were filled with wonder and amazement. "Everyone was filled with awe, and many wonders and miraculous signs were done by the apostles" (Acts 2:43; NIV).

Indeed, there are many other reasons why Jesus, the perfect representation of our transcendent God performed so many miracles. When He performed creative miracles, He was proving that He was the creator. The supernatural acts of Jesus were also the fulfillment of prophecy, proving that He was the promised Messiah. He did miracles to show that he had the authority to forgive sins and to demonstrate that he had the power to drive out demons. His miracles also showed that the kingdom of God had come. Jesus only did what He saw the Father doing, and in so doing, Jesus brought glory to the Father.

Many struggle, whether it is God's will to heal. The battle is based on the fact that not everyone who prays or is prayed for is healed. The problem is not with God. False conclusions abound when healing does not happen. Many excuses are given thinking we are sparing man of false hope. Many believe that it is God's will for them to have a terminal illness, which is blaming God for the disease. There are a few stories in scripture where God did place something pressing on a person who had committed a very offensive act. If that was the case, where a severe sin was committed, that person must repent for that sin. There are illnesses that are the direct result of sin. If we consume certain substances or participate in certain activities, we are inviting sickness and disease into our bodies. It is not from God. And, if we did sin, Jesus still desires to forgive and heal. He will instruct a person to go and sin no more, in other words, repent. For a child of God in the right relationship with God, sickness is not from God. We need to know the Word of God and avoid human-made excuses for illness.

In Matthew 8:2–3, a man with the dread disease of leprosy said to Jesus, "If you are willing, you can make me clean." Jesus said, "I am willing." God's desire and will is for us to be whole. We are His children, and He would never put sickness on us. A father does not do that to his child, and indeed God, the Father, would not do that. Read Luke 11:11–13: "Which of you fathers, if your son asks for a fish will give him a snake instead? Or if he asks for an egg, will give him a scorpion? If you then, though you are evil, know how to give good gifts to your children, how much more will your Father in heaven give the Holy Spirit to those who ask him?"

I love the verse in the gospel of John in which Jesus says, "The thief comes only to steal and kill and destroy; I have come that they may have life, and have it to the full" (John 10:10; NIV).

Sickness is from the thief, and health is from Jesus. Jesus also taught us to pray for His will to be done on earth as it is in heaven. Will there be sickness in heaven? Absolutely not! We always pray for healing, knowing it is God's will. Read the gospels and notice the words of Jesus. Did He ever say that He would not heal someone? It states that He healed all who were brought to Him or encountered Him. He was beaten, taking the stripes for our healing. The Bible says, "By His stripes, we are healed" (1 Peter 2:24, Isa. 53:5; NKJV). Therefore He would never do the opposite, which would undo His stripes and suffering.

I know the question remains: why are some not healed? I already mentioned two standard blocks to healing. Lack of forgiveness and lack of faith; now, I add the absence of the knowledge of God, knowing God, to the list of primary blocks. In addition, the Bible explicitly states that if we do not forgive someone, we will not be forgiven. Healing also requires forgiveness (James 5:16). To have faith for healing, we need to have full knowledge of our heavenly Father. Trust and relationship precede miracles. We need to know who He is to understand who we are in Him and

He in us. We need knowledge of the scriptures to have absolute confidence in believing Jesus wants to and will heal.

Faith is mentioned frequently in scripture. Faith springs forth from intimacy with the Lord. Confidence comes from knowledge of the Lord, not just knowing about Him, but knowing Him intimately. This is not a "name it and claim it" deal, rather genuine faith results in healing. Healings come from an intimate relationship with the Lord and knowing God. The reason for the baptism in the Holy Spirit is to aid in a deep love for the Lord. If a person has unique gifting in a healing ministry, that anointing comes from the Holy Spirit, not man. We follow Jesus's instruction because we love Him, not for our glory. We pray for healing in the name of Jesus and for His glory.

The Teaching of Jesus and the Apostles

As disciples and followers of Jesus, we are given authority to heal the sick of all kinds of diseases, to cast out devils, and to preach the gospel to the poor and the oppressed. Let us observe the ministry and teaching of Jesus on the work of the Holy Spirit as we read John 14, 15, and 16 and the Great Commission in Matthew 28, where Jesus says, "All authority in heaven and on earth has been given to me. Therefore, go and make disciples of all nations." He did the same when He sent out the twelve and then the seventy-two. Putting it all together, He is telling us He has given us the power of the Holy Spirit; therefore, go and do the works I have done. The Great Commission in the Gospel of Mark reads:

> Go into all the world and preach the good news to all creation. Whoever believes and is baptized will be saved, but whoever does not believe will be condemned. And these signs will accompany

those who believe: In my name they will drive out demons; they will speak in new tongues; they will pick up snakes with their hands; and when they drink deadly poison, it will not hurt them at all; they will place their hands on sick people, and they will get well. (Mark 16:15–18; NIV)

What is not often understood is that we need to take authority over sickness, commanding it to go in the name of Jesus. People think we are telling God what to do rather than telling the disease to leave, requiring the body to line up with the will of God. As Peter said, "In the name of Jesus, walk" (Acts 3:6).

The topic of healing is extensive. There is much to learn. There are complications like generational sins and overcoming the vast number of lies from the enemy, which have been accepted for centuries. That is why the other gifts of the Holy Spirit must accompany the gifts of healing for the greatest success in the ministry of healing. It is more than merely having enough faith as though we are to work up faith. It is in knowing Jesus, who must be the object of our faith, our trust in Jesus resulting from knowing who Jesus is and who we are in Jesus, which leads to confidence for healing. Jesus certainly had enough faith, yet the Bible says in Matthew 13:58 that in His home town of Nazareth, "He did not do many miracles there because of their lack of faith." They did not know Him, who He was. They lacked a relationship with Him.

Few have studied scripture in depth, concerning the gifts of healing. When we do study, we must allow the Holy Spirit to be our only teacher. We must have a willing heart and be diligent in our quest, not for head knowledge but for an enlarged heart after God. We do not chase after miracles but resolutely go after God and the advancement of His kingdom of which miracles are a part.

I am not sure the human mind can comprehend all the Word of God has to say concerning signs, wonders, and miracles. It will require an outpouring of the Holy Spirit as prophesied in Joel 2 and quoted by Peter in chapter 2 of the Acts of the Apostles. The other gifts of the Spirit, like knowledge and wisdom, will enhance the gifts of healings.

To confidently pray, we need to know that every promise in His Word is for us. And it is for us now! The gospel is both the spoken message and the demonstration of power for it to be fully preached.

> Yet I dare not boast about anything except what Christ has done through me, bringing the Gentiles to God by my message and by the way I worked among them. They were convinced by the power of miraculous signs and wonders and by the power of God's Spirit. In this way, I have fully presented the gospel of Christ from Jerusalem to Illyricum. (Rom. 15:18–19; NLT)

Notice the expression "fully preached the gospel of Christ." It also says that it is accomplished in word and deed. The gospel is always to be proclaimed fully with words and demonstrations of power. Preaching and the display of authority are consistent throughout the New Testament and accomplished through the Holy Spirit. The kingdom of God is in the Holy Spirit (Rom. 14:17).

Points to consider:

1. Miracles are God's idea and come from Him.
2. Miracles are to glorify God.

3. Miracles confirm the Word of God.
4. Miracles are commanded by Jesus (Luke 9:1, 2).
5. Miracles are promised by Jesus (John 14:12–14).

CHAPTER 14

BE A WITNESS

"Go into all the world and preach the Good News to everyone" (Mark16:15; NLT).

W hy is the baptism in the Holy Spirit so essential to God the Father and Jesus, His Son? First and foremost, it is God's greatest desire to provide the highest level of intimacy possible with the ones He created in His image. Such intimacy is not grasped until experienced. Second, it is so important because it gives us the power to share the gospel with others with whom He also desires a deep relationship. The Spirit produces a loving boldness in our testimony that the mind cannot comprehend, providing supernatural words of knowledge from the Spirit.

First, we are to love the Lord our God with all our heart, soul, mind, and strength, and then to love others as ourselves. Those are the two greatest commandments. His desire is not only for you to be in intimacy with Him but for others to come into intimacy with Him as well. He died for the whole world, all people, regardless of their origin or past lifestyles. Even if you are living in blatant sin, He loves you beyond comprehension. He loves everyone beyond our wildest imagination, hoping His kindness will lead each one into surrendering their life to Him so that He can have fellowship with everyone. Jesus gave us what we call the Great Commission to go into the entire world with the gospel. His final instructions are given to us as follows: "Do not leave Jerusalem, but wait for the gift my Father promised, which you have heard me speak about. For John baptized with water, but in a few days, you will be baptized with the Holy Spirit" (Acts 1:4–5; NIV).

The eleven disciples tried to change the subject, but Jesus continued in His final instructions. "But you will receive power when the Holy Spirit comes on you, and you will be my witnesses in Jerusalem, and in all Judea and Samaria, and to the ends of the earth" (Acts 1:8; NIV). The power of the Holy Spirit in witnessing cannot be explained but is real and observable.

Immediately after speaking these words, Jesus was taken up into heaven before their very eyes. Jesus, with full knowledge of leaving His disciples, intentionally chose these words as His last. Jesus's most significant concern was for them to receive the power to continue His kingdom ministry. Notice the order of His instructions, which followed. They were to be baptized in the Holy Spirit and then to be His witnesses.

We need to follow the same order. We first need the power to be a witness. Then we can witness the way He designed us to testify in the power and giftedness of the Spirit. As we continue through the book of Acts, we notice the power is in both words and deeds. Their speech could convict and convince others of the need to have Jesus in their hearts. The acts of miracles and healings were done by the Spirit to affirm the truth of the spoken words. I sense Jesus asking, do we attempt to witness without the power and manifestation of the Spirit?

To be His witness means to share what He did in your life through the gospel. All who have Christ living in them must tell their story of how it happened and share what changes occurred in their life as a result of coming into relationship with Christ. Telling your story is easy and the most powerfully convicting story anyone can share. No one needs to have a vast knowledge of the Bible or be able to preach a sermon. There is tremendous power in your testimony. "They overcame him (Satan) by the blood of the lamb and by the word of their testimony; they did not love their lives so much as to shrink from death" (Rev. 12:11; NIV).

That verse shows the power in your testimony. If your salvation story can defeat Satan, nothing can stop you from sharing effectively. Most are fearful of sharing their testimony. Fear is a liar and directly from the enemy. We need to overcome fear in the name of Jesus. Of course, the enemy doesn't want us to be a witness, spreading God's love. Satan hates God and His followers. Satan goes around like a roaring lion seeking to devour someone (1 Pet. 5:8). Satan plans to steal, kill, and destroy (John 10:10). But, there is power in the blood of Jesus and your testimony, and we can overcome fear.

You may question, how do I witness? First, share how Jesus called you to Himself, share how you surrendered your life to Him, and then how it changed and blessed your life. That is always safe to do since no one can argue with your experience. But you do not want to stop with your story. Ask if they have received Jesus in their hearts or if they know the Lord in a personal way. If a person does not know the Lord, then ask if they would like to have a relationship with the Lord. If they would, you should lead them in a prayer to repent and receive Jesus. Nothing is more exciting than to lead someone to Jesus.

There are some handy tools to have in your toolbox for winning souls. There are the "Four Spiritual Laws" by Campus Crusade, the "Roman Road" using select verses in the book of Romans, "Evangelism Explosion" by D. James Kennedy, and "Four Steps to Peace with God" by Billy Graham. All of these are very easy for ordinary people to use. I copied the "Four Spiritual Laws," which is the same as "Four Steps to Peace with God" in the cover of one of my Bibles. Later, I transferred the four steps into the scriptures so that I was always using my Bible to share the gospel.

The first verse was John 3:16, which is very popular and easy to remember. Then in the margin or top of the page, I wrote the next verse, John 10:10. With those two verses, I share that God loves them and has a beautiful plan for their life. That covers Law One. In the margin by John 10:10, I wrote the next verse that I needed to use, Romans 3:23, stating that we have all sinned and fall short of God's requirements, which is law two. I would continue in the same manner through all four laws, which are the gospel in a nutshell.

Law three explains that God's only provision is through His Son, Christ Jesus. The Bible says in Romans 6:23, "The wages of sin is death, but the free gift of God is eternal life in Christ Jesus our Lord." This law is indeed the good news that we, as fallen creatures, may have the gift of eternal life. The fourth law explains that we must personally receive the gift of salvation by faith through repentance and inviting Jesus into our hearts. After sharing the four spiritual laws, you ask them if they would like to receive Christ into their hearts. If the response is "yes," then lead them in a prayer to receive Christ. If the answer is "no," further ministry may be needed now or later and will vary according to reasons given. The response of various excuses is where Evangelism Explosion does an excellent job. The more tools you have available, the better. But the best tool is to know what your Bible says.

It is straightforward and such a joy to share the gospel with anyone willing to listen, and it is surprising how many people desire to hear the Good News. The Holy Spirit's job is to convict and convince people of the need for Christ. It is our job to share our story along with the gospel. The first time I used the "Four

Spiritual Laws" was at a county fair where Campus Crusade had a tent set up with music playing, inviting young people to come in for refreshments. We would encourage them to sit down at a table and visit. After introducing ourselves and talking a while, we would ask if they heard of the "Four Spiritual Laws." The answer would nearly always be "no." The "Four Spiritual Laws" came in little booklets, about two inches high and four inches wide, published by Campus Crusade. We would take them through the four laws and ask if they would like to receive Christ. If they prayed with us to receive Jesus, they would get further instruction on receiving and being filled with the Holy Spirit.

My first experience happened when a young man about seventeen years old walked into the tent. He was by himself, so I introduced myself and began visiting. I offered him some refreshments and sat down at a table with him. After visiting, I explained that we were with Campus Crusade and were very excited to provide the best news anyone could receive. I asked if he ever heard of the Four Spiritual Laws, and he said, "No." After going through the booklet with him, I asked if he would like to receive Christ into his heart. He said, "Yes." I was so surprised that I almost said, "No kidding?" We prayed together as I led him to invite Jesus into his heart, and then I went through the last page in the booklet on the Holy Spirit. After he left, I thought, *how could it be that easy*?

Later three younger boys came into the tent in a group. They were maybe fourteen-year-olds, and all went to the same church. I went through the same procedure with them as a group. After presenting the gospel with the Four Spiritual Laws, I asked them individually if they would like to receive Christ into their lives. All three said, "Yes." Again, we prayed as each invited Christ into their hearts. What excitement! How crazy is it that on the first time doing this, it was four for four. I was hooked. That night before retiring, with a big smile on my face, I was asking the Lord, "Did you give me easy ones the first time just to encourage me?" I received no answer, but I was sure He did.

In the future, there were many opportunities to witness individually and to groups. Youth groups from many churches invited me to speak on the second coming. Every time I did, I would share my testimony in closing and give the invitation to receive Christ. I also went on many Lay Witness Missions to various churches, some at a distance. A Lay Witness Mission was a team of people willing to go out to churches to share their testimonies and provide music for the weekend as a revival time in churches. I would usually be assigned to be the last to participate in the Sunday morning service, which would be the last service for the weekend. I would sing "The King Is Coming" after sharing my testimony. It was amazing to watch people's faces and expressions, some with tears, as the Holy Spirit worked in people's lives as I shared my story and sang. After me, the director would speak and give the alter call. Many would come to Christ on such weekends, resulting in revival in many churches.

There was also a Lay Witness Mission II, which was a follow-up to the first one with an emphasis on the Holy Spirit. I did a few of those weekends, sharing my testimony on the baptism in the Holy Spirit. On one occasion, the pastor objected strongly to the baptism in the Holy Spirit after salvation. Simultaneously, a young woman experienced a seizure of some type, making a commotion as she lay on the floor. With the help of other team members, we took her into another room. In my spirit, I knew this was a spiritual attack. I prayed over the lady having the seizure and commanded the evil spirit to leave in the name of Jesus, and immediately she relaxed. Looking at me, she smiled and said she was okay. We need to be ready for attacks from the enemy when sharing the power of the Spirit. The devil will not just sit by. He will react in some way.

As the word got around that I was willing to share my story, various invitations would come to me. I was also invited to lead the local Youth for Christ (YFC) chapter in the Sioux Center high school, where I was teaching. I wanted to be sure that the Lord wanted me to lead YFC because it was a significant commitment meeting every Sunday evening after all churches finished their activities. The area YFC director was leading the chapter in our school as well as in another school. After his invitation, I decided to give it a try, asking the Lord to use me in reaching a few kids for the Lord if He wanted me to lead our YFC. I shared my testimony with about seventy-five students in a private home, and thirty-six students committed their lives to Christ that evening. It was apparent the Lord answered my prayer beyond anything I could have asked for or imagined. I had all the conviction I needed to realize that I must continue.

As the word about YFC spread, many different students from our school began to attend. Every year, new students entered high school, exposing new students to the gospel. We discussed many topics, such as dating, friends, salvation, and other issues. At times, I traded with leaders in other schools, offering me opportunities to share with students in many different schools. Most of the time, I would speak on a topic and follow up my talk with the invitation to surrender their life to Jesus. With some issues, the proper response would be to commit an unsurrendered area of their life or a rededication of their life. There would always be a number of responses. Sometimes ten or more, some evenings two or three, some meetings five or six students would commit their lives to the Lord. Over the years, there were a lot of students who gave their lives to Christ.

There were many other opportunities to share my story, such as Bible studies in homes, teaching Sunday School, special meetings of clubs, employee groups, and AWANA. One of the most significant lessons learned in all of my opportunities to share was the time I directed a seventh- and eighth-grade, one-week Bible Camp at Inspiration Hills. The second to the last night, I planned to speak on giving your life to Christ with the invitation for students to ask Jesus into their lives. I always prayed privately for the working of the Holy Spirit before giving the call for people to surrender their lives to Christ. I prayed, "Lord, I ask for just about every student to give their life to you tonight." I didn't know if I dared to ask for all, so I prayed for just about all. Upon giving the call to surrender their lives to the Lord, every kid but one came forward. When I saw the one who did not come forward, I immediately experienced sorrow and conviction for the lack of my prayer. I asked for forgiveness in my thinking that it might be too much to ask for every student. The one student troubled me greatly.

I desired so much for the young boy who didn't come forward to give his life to Jesus that I visited with him for quite some time on several occasions after that. He never did receive Jesus at the camp, but hopefully, he did later. I got a firm conviction; I was to ask for all to surrender their lives to the Lord, not just most. I didn't know if I should be that bold to pray for all of them to receive. However, the Lord desires for us to be bold and confident. Jesus died for all, so ask for all to experience salvation because Jesus said, "It is not His will that any should perish, but everyone to come to repentance" (2 Pet. 3:9).

Therefore, praying for all to be saved is to pray in the will of the Father and the Son. Never underestimate the power of the Holy Spirit when praying in God's will.

There will be times in witnessing and sharing the gospel that people genuinely receive the Lord into their hearts, and you will, by observation, often be able to tell if it was real. It is always important to follow up whenever possible because, according to the Bible, there are four different kinds of hearts, and only one of those four is the right heart. The Bible illustrates every type of heart in the Parable of the Sower. Read the story in Matthew 13:1–9, and the interpretation of the parable is in verses 18–23. The four different soils are the four different types of hearts of those who hear the gospel. Every person is one of the four soil types.

Some hear the Word only in a natural way, and the devil quickly steals the message away so that it never takes root at all. They are like the hard path where the seed never has the chance to germinate. They have hearts that have been hardened and will not receive the Word. Hardened hearts are incapable of understanding the gospel. You will encounter such souls as you witness. Only God can soften hearts over time, and that is possible as friends and loved ones persist in prayer. Most need to hear the gospel message a number times before their hearts are softened and surrender to Jesus.

Second, some have hearts like rocky soil where the seed takes root quickly but also dried up soon as the hot sun dries up the shallow soil. The seed germinates, but the hot sun scorched the plants, which withered in the shallow soil. Such a heart receives the Word with joy, but it only lasts a short time. The Bible says that it dries up when trouble or persecution comes, and he quickly falls away. Difficulties and persecution originate from the devil and are some of his favorite strategies on people who receive the Word.

Third, some seeds fall in soil among thorns. The seed is your testimony. The soil is the heart that is to receive. The worries and the struggles in this life to obtain wealth choke out the growing seed. Thorns are another strategy the evil one uses to destroy the seed, which germinated and took root. It is so easy to get caught up in our work, trying to make ends meet. There are many concerns, including ministry, which can consume our attention, and we forget about the Lord. The Lord and our relationship with Him must be number one.

Fourth, there is good soil. This heart receives the word and understands it. The gospel takes deep root, resulting in obedience following the Lord. The seed sown in the good soil produces a crop of thirty times as much as was sown and sometimes sixty times or one hundred times the seed planted. The excellent heart represents one who sows more seed through witnessing and leading others to Christ. What would the world be like if each Christian led thirty, sixty, or one hundred souls into the kingdom? How many who call themselves Christian have never witnessed and prayed with just one person to receive Christ? Every person who calls themselves Christian needs to ask, what kind of soil am I? How many have I led to the Lord? Am I the good soil? If not, your relationship with Jesus needs to be in question. We need to consider the words of Jesus personally as well as having this awareness when sharing Christ.

It is always necessary to follow up when we lead someone to Christ. We need to do life with the ones we point to the Lord. Sometimes we need to do a little cultivating of the soil, the heart. When troubles and persecution come, we need to provide counsel to those people. When the cares of this world get too heavy, we need to help bear the load and walk with others. There are many rocks and thorns in this life. We need to be sensitive to the hurts and temptations of others, loving others as ourselves.

There is great joy in leading others to Christ Jesus. Whenever I hear someone's story of hearing the gospel and receiving Christ, it chokes me up at a minimum and usually brings tears of joy. Each one of us needs to share the gospel. I have heard the excuse: I don't have the gift of evangelism. You don't need the gift of evangelism like Billy Graham, but you must witness of Jesus coming into your life. You only need to share your story, using that to present the gospel, inviting people to allow Christ entrance into their hearts. We must go into the whole world as a witness and bear fruit. If we do not, people will go to hell, and it will be our fault. Listen to the word of the Lord to the prophet Ezekiel:

> Now it came to pass at the end of seven days that the word of the Lord came to me, saying, "Son of man, I have made you a watchman for the house of Israel; therefore hear a word from My mouth, and give them warning from Me: When I say to the wicked, 'You shall surely die,' and you give him no warning, nor speak to warn the wicked from his wicked way, to save his life, that same wicked man shall die in his iniquity, but his blood I will require at your hand. Yet, if you warn the wicked, and he does not turn from his wickedness, nor from his wicked way, he shall die in his iniquity; but you have delivered your soul." (Ezek. 3:16–19; NKJV).

God is serious about the baptism in the Holy Spirit so that we are empowered to be His witness in both word and deed to the whole world. If Christ lives in us, the Holy Spirit will naturally give us a burden for the lost. It is a real joy to share Christ in a world that desperately needs and, in many cases, desires Him, but does not have the knowledge of what to do. We will witness out of love for Christ and others. We have a fantastic privilege to serve with the Lord. Do you have a passion for souls? It is essential.

Questions to consider:

1. How comfortable are you in sharing your testimony? How about little parts to start sharing?
2. Do you understand the power in sharing your testimony (read Rev. 12:11)?

CHAPTER 15

FOLLOWING JESUS
❧

"Come, follow me, and I will make you fishers of men"
(Mark 1:17; NIV).

T he contents of this book are the instructions given in scripture
for New Testament initiation or entrance into the Kingdom
of God. When the Holy Spirit calls us, we are to repent, seek
forgiveness, and invite Jesus into our hearts. Then we are to be
baptized in water by another entirely devoted follower of Jesus.
After a person has repented, believed in the Lord Jesus, and has
been baptized, the apostles insisted people be filled or baptized in
the Holy Spirit. But, this is only the beginning of our walk with
the Lord and indeed not an arrival. There is so much more in following Jesus and believing in the Lord Jesus.

The working of the Holy Spirit after receiving salvation is a
continually increasing growth in a process often called sanctifica-
tion (1 Thess. 5:23). As long as we are in this body, we have not
arrived. This life is only the beginning of an exciting journey. I
will cover a few of the many adventures that follow. Walking with
Jesus continually brings new and exciting challenges to life. Many
privileges become yours in entering the kingdom as the disciples

laid out in the book of Acts. You come into a relationship with the most exciting and contagious person known to humanity—Jesus.

First Love

Jesus is a lover like no other, and when you fall in love with such a person, there is an unquenchable fire in your innermost being burning for more. When entering into such a relationship, we live, eat, and sleep, Jesus. That all-consuming relationship is called first love (Rev. 2:4). Your first love is intense and completely occupies your thoughts. When a person experiences salvation, deliverance, and healing, it is impossible to avoid feeling appreciation and gratitude. Receiving Jesus is the most exciting and enjoyable experience known to anyone. It is a complete release from all burdens a person has been carrying. And, it happens when you fully surrender your life to Jesus.

There was a time I lost my first love. It happened to me while taking a course called Bethel Bible, which was an intense course covering the entire Bible. Losing your first love when studying scripture may appear to be strange. How could anyone lose their first love for Jesus when taking a Bible course? I want to show how subtly this can occur. Bethel Bible is not only an intense course but includes much memorization. Several people in the class were brilliant and extremely industrious; the kind of people I enjoy. Being a teacher and these people being graduates of our high school put me in a very competitive position. I was not going to be outdone. I was diligent in memorizing everything to perfection. With all of the mental exercise, my relationship with Jesus gradually began to slip into second place. My relationship with the Lord was waning under such intense study and was annoyingly noticeable.

The decrease in intimacy was so gradual that I didn't recognize how or why it was happening. I realized I was losing relationship, but how could that be. Through the Spirit and the Word, I knew that it was happening and raising my level of concern. The Bible says,

> "But I have this complaint against you. You don't love me or each other as you did at first! Look how far you have fallen! Turn back to me and do the works you did at first. If you don't repent, I will come and remove your lampstand from its place among the churches. (Revelation 2:4–5 NLT)"

Losing your first love is severe to the Lord. It is the first and greatest commandment. I earnestly prayed for revelation as to why this was happening. After approximately one year, the Holy Spirit spoke and revealed that my intellect, my mind, was getting priority over my heart. I needed to take time in knowing the Lord more intimately and enjoying the Lord through reading, meditating, and worshipping the Lord while studying my Bible, not just cramming as much knowledge into my head as possible. I also needed to spend quality time in prayer, listening to His voice, worshipping, and fellowshipping with Him. I needed to take time to love on Jesus.

The solution seemed so simple and easy that I should have been able to figure it out. I asked the Lord why He took so long to tell me that simple solution. His reply was, "I allowed you to struggle so that you would never forget my deepest desire is to have a holy romance with you." I immediately repented, and intimacy returned into my relationship. I know He also desired for me to share that priority of the Lord with others because it is so important to God. I always tell people to study scripture to gain knowledge of the Lord, *to know Him,* and *not necessarily knowing about the Lord.* If our priority is to know Him and love Him, the information about Him will follow with little effort. This awareness is a precious gem in knowing His heart for my heart. What is your priority, head knowledge or heart knowledge? This knowledge is eternally critical. In John 17:3 Jesus says, "And this is eternal life, that they may know You, the only true God, and Jesus Christ whom You have sent."

Many in the church have never experienced knowing the Lord and a first love for Him, which is the first commandment and is eternal life. Experiencing first love, knowing Him, is essential for salvation. When one receives Jesus according to scripture, the Holy Spirit produces a first love for Him.

Worship

A meaningful way to maintain a deep, loving relationship with the Lord is through worship. Scripture gives many ways to worship the Lord, but I want to address intimacy in worship in our church services. We are currently experiencing worship wars in our churches. There is a strong resistance against the more modern worship music on the part of some. New songs spring up continually. Many writers are being inspired to write new music repeatedly. At times, I don't know the song any more than those resisting, but the words are incredibly powerful and worshipful. If the song is unfamiliar, I use the words to worship the living God sincerely, from the heart.

I appreciate how the new songs draw me into the presence of the Lord, deepening my relationship with my creator. The new worship music has taught us how to worship with the older songs as well and made some of the older songs more meaningful. The rediscovery of older songs and the rearrangements of them also contribute significantly to the heart of worship. Songs like "More Love to Thee" can be made into a great worship song. I appreciate it when the worship leaders and writers mix the older songs with some new additions and rework them to be more meaningful, like "Amazing Grace, My Chains Are Gone." We just experienced singing "Joy to the World" for Christmas with minor changes making it a joyful and happy song. They used guitars, drums, keyboard, and arranged it in such a positive way that many were tapping on the pew in front of them. Worship does not depend on the style or instruments used. But, how we sing the songs can undoubtedly aid in heartfelt worship.

Worship has long bordered on entertainment, with special music performed by highly skilled musicians, singing in four parts, producing beautiful harmony, using classical music style, all of which have distracted from the human heart being engaged with God's heart. We focused on performance, singing in parts, making sure we hit the right notes with precise timing. Worship, for the most part, was approaching deadness and nothing more than merely the way we do it. Facial expressions appeared to be bored rather than filled with life and enthusiasm for the Lord. There are still some older people, but very few, who can worship from the heart with older music, but that is almost impossible for the younger generations who do not understand King James language or the use of poetry in the wording. They don't talk that way, so they don't sing that way.

I believe the Lord is behind the change taking place in our churches. Many older songs were messages rather than adoration, and God desires us to worship Him. Jesus was very dissatisfied with cold worship when He walked on this earth, and we also need to take the same message to heart. Jesus said, "You hypocrites! Isaiah was right when he prophesied about you: "These people honor me with their lips, but their hearts are far from me. They

worship me in vain; their teachings are but rules taught by men'"
(Matt. 15:7–9; NIV).

Worship must come from the heart, the spirit, rather than doing
it like we always did, out of habit. Jesus said to the woman at
the well in John 4:23–24 (NIV), "Yet a time is coming and has
now come when the true worshipers will worship the Father in
spirit and truth, for they are the kind of worshippers the Father
seeks. God is spirit, and his worshipers must worship in spirit and
in truth."

Acceptable worship comes from the heart, the spirit, the innermost being of humankind. Philippians 3:3 (NIV) gives an added
explanation of this kind of worship. "For it is we who are the circumcision, we who worship by the Spirit of God, who glory in
Christ Jesus, and who put no confidence in the flesh."

In the NIV, when the word *Spirit* is capitalized, it is the Holy
Spirit, and when it is not capitalized, it is the human spirit. Here
it is capitalized, meaning we worship with the Holy Spirit welling
up from our hearts.

Paul gives a detailed account of worship in 1 Corinthians 14,
in particular, worshiping with the Holy Spirit, which is God's
desire. Verses 14 and 15 are of interest. "For if I pray in a tongue,
my spirit prays, but my mind is unfruitful. So what shall I do? I
will pray with my spirit, but I will also pray with my mind; I will
sing with my spirit, but I will also sing with my mind."

Notice that "to put no confidence in the flesh" is the same as
"the mind being unfruitful," and since praying with your spirit is
praying in tongues, so is putting no confidence in the flesh. The
Bible says the flesh, the mind, is unfruitful. Therefore, you cannot
place trust in the flesh, as stated in Philippians 3:3, above. True
worship in spirit and truth is what God desires. The baptism in
the Holy Spirit enables us to worship in the Spirit through praying
and singing in the Spirit.

Jesus is coming back to receive His bride who will be genuinely in love with Him, a bride that will crave being in the worship taking place in heaven. It will be a bride adorning the beauty of Jesus and longing to be in His presence. The book of Revelation describes the awesome worship taking place in heaven. Read chapter 1 to get a picture of Jesus in His glory and then read chapters 4 and 5 to get an idea of worship in heaven. The Psalms give great views of worship as well. David was an exuberant worshiper, who danced mightily before the Lord, and God approved of such worship. There are other forms of worship in scripture, like raising hands, clapping, falling prostrate, and kneeling before the Lord.

Being involved with the charismatic movement of the 1970s, I initially experienced worship in the power of the Holy Spirit at a Charles and Frances Hunter meeting in Sioux Falls, South Dakota. They taught on the gift of the Holy Spirit and the gifts of the Spirit in 1 Corinthians 12. The teaching was preceded and concluded with a time of worship. During the worship following the preaching, most of the audience broke into singing in the Spirit. Never have I heard such a beautiful sound. The words were in unknown tongues, and the melodies were also in notes given by the Spirit. The harmony was like nothing I heard before, far beyond college choir eight-part harmony. It was a foretaste of what we will experience in heaven.

However, the Bible says that when perfection comes, the gifts will cease, so I'm not sure worship in the Spirit on earth will be witnessed in heaven. Worship in heaven will far exceed worship in the Spirit on earth. The glory of the Lord will be so magnificent that it will no longer compare to worship in the Spirit here on earth and, therefore, will be no longer needed. Our minds cannot fathom what worship will be like in heaven. As described in the Revelation of Jesus, it will be loud and in the presence of holy angels. Imagine it being so stunning that the heavenly beings fall prostrate and cast their crowns at the feet of Jesus. What will we, as humans, do surrounded by such glory? Are you ready for heavenly worship?

We need to get accustomed to long periods of intense worship. We have two Christian colleges in this area, Dordt University in Sioux Center and Northwestern College in Orange City, that decided to break down walls and worship together once a month on Sunday nights. Students plan and lead worship. They have at least one hour of uninterrupted worship and prayer, no sermon, just lifting the name of Jesus and beholding His beauty. It is a pretty awesome experience to worship with them. If we don't like all-out worship, we certainly will not like heaven. Are you anxious and ready for heavenly worship? The Holy Spirit empowers spiritual worship.

Spiritual Warfare

Following Jesus will undoubtedly lead to spiritual warfare. When you believe in the Lord Jesus, you will be delivered from the kingdom of darkness into the kingdom of light, which causes Satan much worry, and he will oppose and contest it. Spiritual warfare may initially sound somewhat frightening, but deliverance is a massive blessing. The Greek word for being saved means saved, healed, and delivered, which is the gift of eternal life; all we need to do is access it. In my lifetime, spiritual warfare was initially acknowledged and addressed in the seventies. It was unheard of before that time.

There are many books written on spiritual warfare, so I will only touch on it briefly to alert readers. If you decide to follow Jesus, you will encounter attacks from the enemy. Some attacks will be subtle, while others may be major. Education on the subject is mandatory, keeping our focus on Jesus, rather than on the devil and his workers. Knowing who Jesus is and who we are in Him eliminates the fear of this topic and an unhealthy obsession over demons. Every Christian needs to know that Jesus defeated the devil on the Cross. However, Satan continues to be extremely deceptive and the most outrageous liar. The only real power he has is our ignorance of his defeat and his tactics.

The name of Jesus is above all names and most powerful. We are to use the name of Jesus in the battle against evil. Knowing Jesus defeated Satan on the cross and that the blood of Jesus is powerful provides us with the needed weapons to overcome the devil. Your testimony, telling what Jesus did for you in delivering you from the kingdom of darkness, is another excellent tool. Jesus endows us with authority over the powers of darkness. Also, remember following salvation, you are a child of God and a joint heir with Jesus. You are seated in the heavenly realms with Jesus (Eph. 2:6) "far above all rule and authority, power and dominion, and every title that is given, not only in the present age but also in the one to come" (Eph. 1:21). Carefully read the book of Ephesians, and it will blow your mind concerning the riches of Christ and our being one with Him, He in us and we in Him.

When Jesus was tempted, immediately following His baptism, He was led into the wilderness to be tempted by Satan. Three times He was tempted, and every time He defeated Satan by the Word of God. Notice Satan also used scripture to tempt Jesus, but Jesus's response was, "the scripture also says." We have God's Word as another weapon against evil and temptation. In Ephesians 6:10–18, we are given the armor of God that we are to put on in defeating darkness. We are to put on the entire armor. We have the command to use the Word of God and to pray in the Spirit. I can testify to the fact that praying in the Spirit is extremely powerful because the Spirit within us is greater than any other power. "The Spirit who lives in you is greater than the spirit who lives in the world" (1 John 4:4; NLT).

Mentioned so far, we already have many weapons with which to come against the evil one. Knowing this should give us confidence, the faith, for deliverance from any besetting sin, illness, addiction, or any other evil with which the enemy has troubled us. Jesus came to destroy the works of the devil; to think otherwise would be unbelief. Any rebuke of the enemy must be spoken out loud and directly to the infirmity. You are not telling God what to do; instead, you are commanding the weakness or stronghold to leave in the name of Jesus. You are commanding your body to line up with God's will. We do not tell God what to do because He owes us nothing. He has already given us the victory in Christ Jesus. We need to declare and use it with unwavering faith. We have been given the authority and need to vocally rebuke all kinds of evil in the name of Jesus.

Persecution

In America, we have no idea of intense oppression. But, throughout the world, there is a lot of severe persecution taking place. There are places where they line up Christians and shoot them. In some areas, they are imprisoned and tortured. The persecution we face in America is primarily being ridiculed or verbally abused, which, coming from friends and family, can be exceedingly hurtful. Whatever form it takes, the Bible assures us there will be persecution. Paul said to Timothy, "Yes, and everyone who wants to live a godly life in Christ Jesus will suffer persecution" (2 Tim. 3:12; NLT).

That verse is in the context of the last days. We also read in the book of Revelation that there will be worldwide persecution before the return of Jesus. Jesus also affirms that in the end times, there will be great persecution.

> Then you will be handed over to be persecuted and put to death, and you will be hated by all nations because of me. At that time, many will turn away from the faith and will betray and hate each other, and many false prophets will appear and deceive many people. Because of the increase of wickedness, the love of most will grow cold, but he who stands firm to the end will be saved. (Matt. 24:9–13; NIV)

There is a special blessing for those who are persecuted and remain faithful to the Lord.

> Blessed are those who are persecuted because of righteousness for theirs is the Kingdom of heaven. Blessed are you when people insult you, persecute you and falsely say all kinds of evil against you because of me. Rejoice and be glad, because great is your reward in heaven, for, in the same way, they persecuted the prophets who were before you. (Matt. 5:10–12; NIV)

Jesus promises that if we share in His suffering, we will also rise with Him. In that sense, we complete the suffering of Christ. This suffering is not from sickness or disease, but suffering for the sake of the gospel and the kingdom of God. It is the same suffering that Jesus experienced. We join ourselves to Him in His pain (1 Pet. 4:12–16), and we are to rejoice in suffering as we bear the name of Christ. The apostles also suffered and counted it all joy. "The apostles left the Sanhedrin, rejoicing because they had been counted worthy of suffering disgrace for the Name" (Acts 5:41; NIV).

If we are in love with Jesus, we will gladly suffer for Him as the apostles did. Are we in love with Him? There will be a unique crown for those who give their lives for the sake of Christ. They will raise loud hallelujahs in heaven as they glorify the Lord of lords and King of kings.

Fruit

Those filled with the Holy Spirit will yield much fruit. Many feel that the fruit of the Spirit is something we have to work hard to produce. That is not the truth. An apple tree does not have to work to create apples instead of peaches; it naturally produces apples. A person in a relationship with Jesus, walking in the Spirit, naturally produces the fruit of the Spirit and not the fruit of the sinful nature. The Holy Spirit in a believer produces the fruit of the Spirit. Without the gift of the Holy Spirit, there will be no fruit.

> When you follow the desires of your sinful nature, the results are very clear: sexual immorality, impurity, lustful pleasures, idolatry, sorcery, hostility, quarreling, jealousy, outbursts of anger, selfish ambition, dissension, division, envy, drunkenness, wild parties, and other sins like these. Let me tell you again, as I have before, that anyone living that sort of life will not inherit the Kingdom of God. But the Holy Spirit produces this kind of fruit in our lives: love, joy, peace, patience, kindness, goodness, faithfulness, gentleness, and self-control. There is no law against these things! Those

who belong to Christ Jesus have nailed the passions and desires of their sinful nature to his cross and crucified them there. Since we are living by the Spirit, let us follow the Spirit's leading in every part of our lives. (Gal. 5:19–25; NLT)

The baptism in the Holy Spirit enables us to walk in the Spirit, making the fruit natural, but without it, it takes much effort.

As believers, we also produce another fruit, and that is the souls of people. Jesus taught with many parables. The parable of the four soils in Matthew 13 is an excellent example of reaching the lost. There is only one good soil, and that one produces another crop of a hundred, sixty, or thirty times what was sown. The four soils represent four kinds of people. How much seed have your sown? Have you produced another crop? I addressed this parable in the chapter on evangelism.

In John 15, the fruit could represent a variety of things. It could represent our character and how we treat others. It is one of the attributes of our relationship with Christ. It can be the souls of people who we won for the kingdom. It also represents our obedience in following the Lord. It is the fruit of being connected to Jesus, the vine, where God is the gardener.

Follow Jesus

I fully realize that the four concepts I have presented in this book are not taught in all churches as the proper and full initiation into the kingdom of God. If God is to fulfill the prophecy in His Word, and I know He certainly will, then before Jesus returns, this must be the direction the bride of Christ will follow. The baptism in the Holy Spirit may seem unnecessary or optional to some but will be essential to survive the days preceding the return of Jesus.

It is also necessary for maximum effectiveness in presenting the gospel and for full intimacy with the Lord.

God is already moving the church in this direction. God is already powerfully pouring out His Spirit in numerous places. As the Spirit is poured out, mighty signs, wonders, and miracles will follow. At the same time, there is going to be a great falling away—the great apostasy. As a result, there will be much resistance to the move of the Spirit. The apostasy is also well underway as the adulterous church becomes more and more liberal. In which camp will you be? There will be much confusion in the end times, as false prophets teach false doctrine. Each person will need to be personally familiar with the Word of God and filled with the Holy Spirit to survive. Read the parable of the ten bridesmaids, in Matthew 25; each person is responsible for obtaining their own oil.

The Bible says there will be many false teachers leading many astray and the love of many will grow cold. Those are chilling thoughts. It also says that if God didn't shorten those days, no one would survive. It will be a time of great distress and persecution worldwide. Read Matthew 24 to get the big picture and then go on to study other related portions of scripture. If there were false teachers, at that time, there will undoubtedly be false teaching before Jesus's return, and it will be received by many. The devil isn't wasting any time. He knows his time is drawing nearer and wants to take as many as he can with him to a horrible Christ-less eternity, so horrific that the human mind cannot comprehend it. Satan began with his lies centuries ago and has continued to this day, building the false church. The only way to know the truth will be to understand the Word of God. Study the scriptures carefully and start now.

My passion for the church and humankind is to know the truth. The battle is over truth. God is the truth. His Word is truth. Jesus, His Son, is truth, and the Holy Spirit is truth. Allowing the Holy

Spirit to lead and guide you into truth is essential. The apostles inform us in the book of Acts what is crucial in kingdom life: receive Jesus into your heart, repent of your sins, be baptized in water, and be baptized in the Holy Spirit. I pray that every person reading this book will experience Christ in deeper intimacy and experience abundant life to the full in Christ. Satan comes to steal, kill, and destroy, but Jesus comes to give life in abundance (John 10:10). We have been given these instructions in the Bible so that we will have a blessed life. Jesus would not have paid such a huge price for the gift of eternal life and the gift of the Holy Spirit if it were not needed and only presented as an option.

The most exciting days for Christians are right at the door. We are living at a time when prophecy concerning the end times is about to be fulfilled as the day of Jesus's return approaches. Every person on earth will personally need to decide if they will be part of the great apostasy or be in the bride of Christ. The end-time outpouring of the Holy Spirit will be as never before. There will be signs, wonders, and miracles as the Spirit manifests itself in the lives of believers. At the same time, false Christs and false prophets will appear and perform great signs and wonders to deceive even the elect—if that were possible (Matt. 24:24). Are you able to distinguish between the two? You will need to understand the Bible and be a devoted follower of Jesus to identify the difference. Read your Bible personally through the lens of the Holy Spirit. Obey and follow Jesus with the help of the Holy Spirit. You will live fulfilled and abundantly. You will be an overcomer.

My Prayer for Each Reader of This Book

I kneel before the Father, from whom his whole family in heaven and on earth derives its name. I pray that out of his glorious riches, he may strengthen you with power through his Spirit in your inner being, so that Christ may dwell in your hearts through faith. And I pray that you, being rooted and established in love, may have power together with all the saints to grasp how wide and long and high and deep is the love of Christ, and to know this love that surpasses knowledge—that you may be filled to the measure of all the fullness of God. Now to him who is able to do immeasurably more than all we ask or imagine according to his power that is at work within us, to him be glory in the church and in Christ Jesus throughout all generations, forever and ever! Amen. (Eph. 3:14–21; NIV)

Questions for discussion:

1. If Jesus were to return right now, would you be satisfied with your life?
2. What would you really like to improve or change?
3. How in love are you with Jesus?
4. Do you have a desire to worship Him, in intimacy, with your whole being?
5. Are you prepared for spiritual warfare? What kind of attacks have you experienced?
6. Are you ready for persecution as Jesus describes in Matthew 24:9–25 before His return?
7. What kind of fruit are you producing? Consider Galatians 5:19–25 and John 15:1–8.
8. Do you desire a deeper, more intimate relationship with the Lord?

9. Are you equipped to identify false teaching of great deception and false prophets performing counterfeit miracles in the end times? Read Matthew 24:4–24 and Revelation 13:13.

10. What chapter or chapters in this book challenged you the most? Explain.

CPSIA information can be obtained
at www.ICGtesting.com
Printed in the USA
FSHW020617071120